MAKING HERSTORY

Voices of the Thwaites and Fitzpatrick Women Across Time and Place

Published by Melbourne Books
Level 9, 100 Collins Street,
Melbourne, VIC 3000
Australia
www.melbournebooks.com.au
info@melbournebooks.com.au

National Library of Australia
Cataloguing-in-Publication entry
Creator: Downey, Helen, author.
Title: Making Herstory: Voices of The Thwaites and Fitzpatrick Women Across Time and Place.
ISBN: 9781922129604 (paperback)
Subjects: Thwaites, Mary Ann.
Thwaites, Mary Ann--Family.
Family secrets--Australia.
Women pioneers--Australia.
Women--Australia--Social conditions.
Other Creators/Contributors:
Secen, Lorraine, author.
Dewey Number: 920.720994

MAKING HERSTORY

Voices of the Thwaites and Fitzpatrick Women Across Time and Place

Helen Downey
with Lorraine Secen

M
MELBOURNE BOOKS

Contents

Acknowledgements

I have such appreciation and admiration for Ethel Thwaites and Theodora Fitzpatrick, the female descendants of pioneers John and Mary Ann Thwaites of Queenscliff, for preserving this cameo of women's activities and thoughts, from early Australian colonisation through to the 1990s.

Heartfelt gratitude to Lorraine Secen, for the foundation research and organisation of the letters, diaries, stories and photos of the Thwaites and Fitzpatrick women, which became the launching pad for this book.

Thank you to Margaret Thwaites, Helen Canale, Helen Moore, Jocelyn Grant, Bill Brown, Jack Beazley, Elizabeth Downey, Sophie Couchman, Philip Maxsted and Kirsty Grant, for providing information and giving generously of their time.

We were fortunate to have the opportunity to interview Nancy Weaver, Theo Fitzpatrick's climbing companion and lifelong friend, who passed away in Hobart on 22 April 2013 at the age of 103.

The Archives Office of Tasmania, Queenscliffe Historical Museum, Queenscliffe Maritime Museum, the National Museum of Australia (People and the Environment Section) and the Ian Potter Centre: NGV Australia have given valued assistance.

We are most grateful to David Tenenbaum, Publisher at Melbourne Books, for his ongoing confidence, patience, guidance and sensitivity. Our capable Editor, Chloe Brien, has earned our respect and admiration throughout the editing process.

The support of the Victorian Women's Trust, led by Executive Director and most valued mentor Mary Crooks, supported by Anne Paul, the Victorian Women's Benevolent Trust Manager, was pivotal to the completion of *Making Herstory: Voices of the Thwaites and Fitzpatrick Women Across Time and Place.*

Helen Downey
14 July 2014

Introduction

The voices of the Thwaites and Fitzpatrick women, from letters, diaries, stories and poetry, reverberate in the empty chasm of unrecorded female experience. There were women, in partnership with men, pioneering the settlements, establishing the services and setting up the administration in the Bellarine Peninsula, as well as performing the groundbreaking work of opening up Tasmania's wilderness to sport and recreation. Straddling two centuries, this book examines the Victorian frontier existence of Mary Ann Thwaites, born in London in 1837; her daughter Ethel, born in Queenscliff in 1875; and the 1940s Tasmanian wilderness expeditions of her granddaughter Theodora Fitzpatrick.

This sea-to-summit story, sifted from the writings of a mother and daughter, has intrigue laced with a surprising literary flavour. Unravelling Ethel's past brings an understanding of why her daughter Theo developed a taste for hiking, mountaineering and skiing, never returning to seaside Queenscliff. Theo wrote:

> There they stand, dreaming one more day of their thousand, thousand years of life: the everlasting hills. Clear in the afternoon light, opalescent in hue, from the outline of the Western Bluff to the classical spires of Mount Ossa, and the faint, but thrilling tracery of the skyline of Frenchman's Cap. From the Cirque one sees the terraced valleys falling, mile on mile to the Forth Gorge, like some gigantic Zanadu pleasure-garden arranged for the delights of gods, not men.

Theodora Ethel Fitzpatrick was born in Queenscliff, Victoria, in 1915, and was raised on the Bellarine Peninsula. In spite of her upbringing at sea level, she emerged as a Tasmanian high country trailblazer in the early 1940s, when she was among the first women to take up the outdoor pursuits of walking, skiing and mountaineering. Lorraine Secen shared a lifelong love of the Tasmanian wilderness with Theo. She inherited her friend's writing, photos and family memorabilia, and approached me to write a biography and fulfil Theo's dream of having her Tasmanian story published.

The formidable feminist, nationalist and author Miles Franklin despaired of women winning an equal place in history, with some very blunt language:

> … the history of Australia was a history of female self-sacrifice. Men were inherently parasitic: 'there never was a man who achieved anything without some woman as potato to his willowslip, but they like to do it without acknowledgment.' Australian women will never win an equal place in history until they ceased to be 'a nation of charwomen'.[1]

Was Franklin correct that the complicity of Australian women kept them subservient and was a significant hindrance in their attainment of equality with men? Or is it a male conspiracy that hides the recorded experience of their mother, wife, daughter or sister? Are female accomplishments, measured against those of men, deemed by society as not worthy of celebration? In the twenty-first century, will progressive publishing of the stories of women turn the tide of centuries of anonymity and the measuring of a woman's worth against standards set by a patriarchal society?

The limiting self-imposed personal boundaries of young women can be traced back to a lack of knowledge of how women have behaved through the ages. Immeasurable loss of the potential to improve the world originates where there is an absence of recorded stories of the lives of women in the formative years of girls. The fragile self-worth of women and girls is damaged again and again when there is an absence of the reporting of women's affairs. Belief by girls and women in their capabilities and potential can be stunted when they are denied stories of the success and achievements of women.

Hadary and Henderson, raising awareness of the perception of women, advocate the education of future leaders:

> Our obligation as women is to ensure that our sons and daughters and the generations of children that they are raising have a very different view of women and their potential in the workforce and contribution in society and the community.[2]

Knowing what was normal in the life of an Australian pioneer woman, and the successive generations of women in her family, is a step in the right direction. This book provides a substantial sense of the times in which these women lived, bringing a precious historical asset into the public gaze. It is merged with narrative in a way that brings the women and their stories to life.

A major hurdle for publication was convincing a publisher that there was a market for a story about women who were 'missing in action' from the history books. The first rejection was from a female publisher, who said matter-of-factly, 'Theodora Fitzpatrick isn't a celebrity. We're not interested.' A publisher friend of a friend wouldn't touch it because Theo wasn't in Wikipedia. A third person claimed interest, but would only come on board if we could prove Ethel Fitzpatrick's writing had literary merit. Should we be surprised? Apparently not, when you examine the findings in *How Women Lead*, published in 2012:

> Despite the positive images of women in corporate leadership tracks, a study from Catalyst found that women worldwide still are not advancing through the pipeline at the same rates as men, even when they have identical credentials, including MBA degrees.[3]

It would appear that women continue to be erased from corporate leadership, and history, by popular consent. How do we eradicate an ingrained mindset that perpetuates inequality? One answer is perseverance to promote and publish *herstories*. You can find them anywhere and everywhere — just keep your eyes, ears and mind open.

Recently, while looking at the Joseph Brown Collection at NGV Australia, I noticed a *herstory* there on the wall:

> The 1920s witnessed the rise in modernism in Australia and it was the commitment of female artists such as Grace Crowley, Margaret Preston and Thea Proctor to working in the modern style that largely shaped the movement. Ironically, they are now considered leaders of the period.
>
> Although women were among the best printmakers in Australia during the inter-war years, with only a few exceptions, their works were ignored or marginalised during their lifetimes. Throughout this period, women artists championed modernism, while male artists predominately continued to work within their nationalistic pastoral landscape tradition.[4]

Making Herstory sets the record straight in a similar way by proving that women were present, that they were making a valuable contribution on the piers of frontier Queenscliff and the peaks of the Tasmanian wilderness. Returning *herstories* to the public domain claims equality for women and signals zero tolerance for the imbalance of female representation in the future.

Chapter 1

Mary Ann and Ethel

There were women on the piers

Thwaites Walk runs along the cliff top, on the edge of Citizens Park, above the Port Phillip Sea Pilot's building in Queenscliff. It was named first and foremost to honour Mayor William J. Thwaites, but such was the contribution of the Thwaites pioneer family of fishermen, boatmen, seamen and building contractors to Queenscliff, it is recorded as being named for all the Thwaites men, who were members of the volunteer lifeboat crews of the past. In the Victorian tradition, the Thwaites women had simply vanished.

Inhumane sailing ship conditions for Mary Ann

The writing of Mary Ann's daughter, Ethel Fitzpatrick (nee Thwaites) is dotted with the 'gold nuggets' of women's lost experience. Ethel was born on 31 July 1875 at Fishermen's Flat, in the town of Queenscliff, spelt without an 'e', in the Borough of Queenscliffe, spelt with an 'e', the smallest borough in Victoria, which includes the towns of Queenscliff and Point Lonsdale and covers only thirteen square kilometres. She was the fifth daughter of John and Mary Ann Thwaites. They lived in the first house built in Fishermen's Flat, in Wharf Street, the closest home to the railway station. These are the words of Ethel, telling the family story of the emigration of the runaway lovers:

My parents came out to Australia in 1858 ... John and Mary Thwaites were married in London at the early age of nineteen and sixteen. Life was too hard for the young weaver, not only in the way of making a living, but the awful conditions of life generally, at that time. Hangings and deportation, for what is now considered trivialities, were a daily occurrence. Crime was rife, crime of all kinds. No woman could go out at night without an escort and young John, after being married a year, decided to emigrate with his wife and newly born son. They had a fearful time on that voyage; storms followed them all the way. They were blown out of their course again and again, and were battened down several times. The baby, John, died and was buried at sea.

. . .

Sitting before a blazing log fire tonight, my mind wanders back over the years when these two, Mary and John, made the then perilous journey to this far-off land of Australia. I recall my mother's story of that long and tedious time of three months duration, so full of anxiety. Storms were encountered that made it more than probable they would never reach their destination.

. . .

We lived in a little seaside town and as a child, for a long time and until I was old enough to understand, my mother told me nothing of her reluctance to sit on the sands or to bathe in the sea. Later, the explanation came. It was that she had buried her firstborn at sea.

In those early Victorian days, girls were married as early as sixteen or seventeen and my mother, whose people were quite comfortably well-off, made a runaway match … with a young weaver who captured her young and unsophisticated heart. I may say here that it lasted a lifetime.

Feeling very much the disapproval of his wife's people, my father began to persuade my mother to emigrate, so it came about that just after her first baby arrived, my mother being then about eighteen years, they embarked on an old ship, the *Africa* … The conditions on board were appalling. No sort of catering was made for young children, let alone young babies, and when I became old enough to know, I felt that my mother's lot was to see her baby gradually starved to death, finally to find a resting place (if one can call it so) in the sea.

Search for missing Thwaites Walk women

Pioneer women documented the hardship, the sheer weight of circumstance, pitted against them. First-generation Australian Ethel Fitzpatrick appeared frustrated by some missing pieces of the Thwaites puzzle at this point in her story.

I often wish I could have known all the circumstances of their early struggles for a place in this undeveloped, strange and primitive country. There was no weaving to be done, and no machinery even set up. What was this tall, fair and broad young man with a wife on his hands to turn to? The first position he found was with a man wanting some help to milk cows. Here, he worked from 'early morn to dewy eve' on a bare pittance. He was persuaded to leave that and take to fishing. All this time, their small stock of money was dwindling and my mother begged him to leave the very small cottage of three rooms and get a tent where they could live cheaper.

...

I wish now that I had taken more notice of the stories told by my parents to the elder ones, who in turn told them to us younger ones, of London their home, of their friends and relations there, to whom they never wrote because of their poverty, their struggle to live. Last night I heard over the air some London street cries, which were very familiar to me, because Father used to amuse the smallest of us in that way. The cat's meat maw particularly amused us, for we could easily imagine everybody's cats sitting on their doorsteps well ahead of the time of the call.

...

They were lured here by the glowing accounts of the wonders of this land. Gold could be picked up in the rough streets, they heard and read. Work was plentiful and it was a place where Jack was as good as his master. I am rather vague about their proceedings when they did eventually arrive in Melbourne. But I know they were almost without funds and the journey to Geelong, where they were advised to go, just about broke them. They got rooms in a little broken down old shack, which a former immigrant had run up for himself, and my father set out to look for work. He found everyone doing the same, but eventually heard of someone at Barrabool Hills who needed a man for milking and general farm work on a place not yet cleared. My Father didn't know one end of a cow from another. He was game enough to try, but the pay was so small they couldn't exist on it.

Hearing that fishing was good at Indented Head, he went there, put up a tent and in it two children were born to them. The fish sold readily enough, when they were plentiful, but when they were scarce times were hard, and it was a long way to take the catch to be sold. So again came a shift, this time to Queenscliff, living in a tent again until money was saved to start building a house. In that tent another son was born. When he became Mayor of Queenscliffe, he used to tell the story on the platform of the hall that doors never bothered him because he was born in a tent, a fact of which he often had to remind his wife when he left all the doors open. This never failed to get a laugh because they did not know it was true and thought it was a good joke.

How well I remember King Billy

When Ethel, the ninth and second-youngest child of John and Mary Ann Thwaites, took on the task of writing the family history, she delivered a rich slice of early Queenscliff. Her descriptions of the industrious and mostly respected Chinese fishermen, along with her mother's recollections of local Indigenous tribal leader King Billy, throw new light on the everyday challenges of pioneer women.

As things improved, my parents re-moved to Queenscliff, where the remaining seven children were born. The family comprised six daughters and three sons, the latter all becoming good businessmen in owning their own businesses, and the girls marrying more or less efficient men, quite comfortably off. In those early days, I have heard my mother speak of the fear in which many of her days were passed, fears for the safety of her young children when my father and elder brothers were out fishing. With a black's camp on one side of our home and a Chinese camp on the other, one can guess of the anxiety of a mother when knives were drawn and a free fight between the two factions took place. Behind locked and barricaded doors, the clash of battle, the war cries of the blacks mixed with the excited chatter of the Chinese were heard with bated breath, and relief when by degrees the noise died down.

Our home, however, was never molested. Mother thought it was due to the fact that she had often explained to the Aborigines, who from time to time asked her for 'baccy', that she could only give them a little.

'No money,' she would reiterate, until they would grin and go away.

A little tea or sugar she would always manage to give them. As only one at a time came, it was rather a good bit to be giving away: hence the small amounts. How well I remember King Billy, who wandered around, a lonely figure with all his tribes scattered and stories told of the corroborees they had where the railway station now stands.

Fred: Favourite of the Fishermen's Flat Chinese

The Chinese were among the first fishermen to arrive in Queenscliff in the 1860s. They were soon joined by commercial fishermen camping on the sand flats near their boats and Queenscliff's first jetty, until complaints about their 'squatting' led to allotments being surveyed and leased to licensed fishermen and their families. The same year that Ethel was born, her father John Thwaites, a pioneer Queenscliff fisherman, began paying rates for a cottage in Wharf Street, on land owned by the Crown, known as Fishermen's Flat.[1] Ethel is believed to be the first of the Queenscliff Thwaites not to be born in a tent, although it seems likely that the family was occupying the land that became Allotment 1 well before licensing began, and purchased a licence when the licensing system was introduced.[2]

Queenscliff was one of numerous Victorian country towns settled by large numbers of Chinese people:

> A typical Chinese camp had its own stores, joss-house, cookshop, lottery houses, fan-tan rooms and brothels, its streets and lanes lined with brick, weatherboard, iron and canvas dwellings. Usually built on cheaper low-lying ground … The Chinese themselves were peaceable and law abiding, but the women of the camps, some married, but more of them prostitutes and almost entirely European, were frequently in court on charges …[3]

An invitation to Ethel's eldest brother to join in a Fishermen's Flat Chinese ceremonial celebration is evidence of the generally harmonious relationship between the Queenscliff pioneers and the early Chinese population. Her mother was typical of the day, with her distrust of foreigners.[4] But her father, a former skilled weaver, like many others became a fisherman out of necessity and had everything to learn from the time-tested traditions of the Chinese fishermen. Interestingly, reports of anti-Chinese activity brought a rebuke from the visiting Commissioners of the Imperial Chinese government in 1887, when they were presented with a petition by Melbourne Chinese leaders, which included their objections to unprovoked and cowardly assaults on tea and vegetable sellers by 'the young and simple'.[5]

Ethel's brother Alfred, referred to as Fred, features in her colourful recollection of an early Australian multicultural community in the melting pot of Queenscliff.

The Chinese camp was the worst menace. They were so terribly excitable, knives would appear as if from nowhere, although if there were any casualties we children did not know it. My eldest brother Fred was a general favourite among them, and they liked and trusted him. I remember his telling us that in playing a practical joke on them he was at one time in danger of his life. He was invited to a religious ceremony to be held in a big tent at their camp. This was a great honour and showed that they liked and trusted Fred, who was very ill-advised to take the principal part in this affair.

I cannot remember all the details, but the principal facts were that the Chinese were sitting on stools placed in a circle, with the principal officiating in the centre. Before the ceremony began, Fred moved from stool to stool and surreptitiously slipped a noose of string, which was passed under the canvas to him, under the legs of the stools. His fellow conspirators being able to tell where to place them by seeing his shadow inside the lighted tent, which of course was very different in dress and outline to that of the Chinese for them to distinguish.

When the opportune time arrived, he was to give the signal, which was a sharp tug on the string, or light rope as it really was. This came when all the Chinese, at a given low command, leaned forward to put their mouths to small bowls of some thick sweet stuff. At the same time, the lights were extinguished in some way I have forgotten. The next beggars description: knives of course were out, chattering and threatening filled the air. My brother often told us how lucky it was for him that it was dark, otherwise there isn't the slightest doubt he would have been stabbed to death by one hundred knives.

Fortunately, when a light was procured, Fred was close to an old Chinaman called Old One-eye (on account of his having only one eye), with whom Fred was a special favourite. Also Fred had taken the precaution to be covered, as they were, with the stuff they were to drink. Even at such a critical time, he was amused at their appearance. With liquid all over their faces and running down their beards, they looked so funny. Not that he wanted to laugh at the time, tho' later on as children we remember hearing him suddenly burst into a fit of laughter at the remembrance.

Old One-eye and Fred's ruse of not attempting to run away eventually pacified them. The old man spoke to the officiating Chinese, who calmed the others and allowed One-eye to question my brother.

'You not do this thing, my son?'

'Do you think I would take part in your sacred ceremony, and get covered in all this muck, and take part in a trick against you, a friend of mine?' he returned.

'He do it alright!' they screamed in his face.

Outwardly calm, but with his heart thumping against his ribs, my brother stood in their midst.

Eventually, their leader told him to go out quietly and if any molested him, he would deal with them later. Five minutes later my brother was in bed with cold-water cloths on his head, Mother giving him weak brandy and water. That was Fred's first and last attempt at practical joking in the Chinese camp.

...

These Chinamen used to catch a horrible-looking white octopus thing with lots of tentacles, called squid. They dried the squid, packed it in barrels and sent it to the Chinese in the goldfields. It became a gambling hell, and worse, for several abandoned white women lived there and eventually they were ordered out of Queenscliff, which was a tremendous relief to the women of this ever-growing town.

Risky business navigating The Rip

For the fishermen, boatmen and sea pilots' wives there was ever-present anxiety: the sea that gave them their livelihood also took lives. The worst disaster ever to hit Port Phillip Sea Pilots occurred on the morning of 15 July 1873.[6] A pilot and three crewmen were drowned when the pilot schooner *Rip* was hit by a huge wave while sailing through Port Phillip Heads. Pilot John McKenzie left behind a widow with five children. Exactly a month after the disaster, on 15 August 1873, the Thwaites' eighth child, James, was born.

What excitement there was when the fishermen's pier was built! My brother told me how thankful the fishermen were to be able to moor their boats near it and to tie their dinghies to it. These dinghies were small boats used to row off to the larger ones. They were days full of anxiety, as there were no engines in the boats as there are today. Depending on sail, as they were, it was quite a risky business to navigate The Heads, or The Rip, as it was called, and scarcely a house that either a father or brother was not drowned. When a sudden storm arose, the women would gather anxiously on the pier and as boat after boat returned, they who returned were gladly welcomed back. But it often happened that one boat did not return.

I shall never forget how we children would go past the fishermen's cottages and count those who would never return. In a row of ten cottages, eight people were missing. One of the pictures that pass before my mind tonight is of a broad, heavily built man with a pleasant face. He had a wonderful deep bass singing voice, and people in the little church listened with delight to the rolling notes that were like notes played on an organ. He was trying to return home through The Rip with his two sons when the boat was struck by a squall and almost overturned.

The father was washed overboard and carried by a huge wave onto a ledge of rock. He was seen upon the rock for an instant, then a recurring wave washed him again into the sea. The boys were unable to get near the rock and had to watch their father for the second time washed onto the rock. He stood upright and sang the first few bars of 'Home At Last', before he disappeared forever. Such disasters often occurred and our anxiety about our own folk may be guessed at. We were a fortunate family in that regard, and they always returned safely.

. . .

In addition to the perils of fishing in those far-off days, there was the job of meeting the mail steamers. A boat, called The Doctor's Boat, put off from what was also called The Doctor's Jetty to pick up the mail brought from overseas by vessels too big to call at the pier, to be sent to Melbourne from Queenscliff by train. On pitch-black nights, with the wind howling and a raging high sea running, several men would set out on this perilous trip in the small boat. Father was one of those whose duty it was to do this work, and I recall how Mother would see to it that we younger ones went off to bed early so that she would not be irritable with us in her anxiety. The older ones understood and would quietly read or sew. Elizabeth, the sister next oldest to myself, often thought it to be much better if they quietly chatted, to help pass the time away until Father's return, but Mother preferred to follow him in imagination on that journey.

It was dangerous work, with the mail in large bags, hooked on long ropes and lowered into the small boat tossing alongside. Exactly how this was managed I do not know, for Father objected to the little ones in the family made unduly anxious. Besides, I was at that time a sleepwalker and they did not wish to unduly excite me. It has just come to my mind that when my life became more active and I was old enough to think of and act for others, that dangerous habit ceased.

I remember Father telling us about the building of the fort and barracks at Queenscliff, and how one night, in returning from the trip to the mail-boat, he was pushing his way through the bushes, when he cannoned into what seemed to be a body, but he couldn't understand how it moved away and came back. To his horror, it proved to be a man hanging there. He reported it immediately and could never understand that there was no enquiry and the incident seemed more like some horrible nightmare than reality, except for the fact that he took whoever was in authority to the spot and showed where the body hung. Father always thought it was a Negro, but Mother said that was most likely that the face would have turned black with suffocation, which did seem the most likely explanation.

Chapter 2

Ethel

Living in Queenscliff when feminism was a luxury

While the act of combining the autobiographical recollections and recovering the lost experience of a mother and daughter challenged the patriarchal mindset that omitted women from historical records, I discovered that just being a woman didn't equip me to speak as a woman. Somehow, I had to unravel the experiences of the Thwaites and Fitzpatrick women, to contribute to the collective memories of 'every woman'. This definition of feminist readings of male and female texts by Frances Devlin-Glass and Annette Comte highlights the differences:

> If feminist readings of male texts suggest the need for an adversarial approach to disrupt the process of emasculation, the reading of female texts is driven by the need to connect with or to recuperate the context and traditions that link women together.[1]

Having trained as a volunteer heritage guide, perhaps I was too well-practised at presenting the male view of the history of Queenscliff. Had there been any female traditions linking women together in this seaside town?

Anne Longmire explained the concept of the 'New Woman' that was emerging around the 1890s, in her book on the Catalyst Club that formed in the first years of the twentieth century:

> This type contested the ideology of womanhood, made incursions into male territory, yet was never seen in the vernacular of the day as a 'mannish feminist', in regard to charm, personal elegance, intelligence and often devoted maternity.

It would take a few decades before Fishermen's Flat or Queenscliff spawned a feminist, but meanwhile Longmire noted, 'The Austral Salon of Melbourne was likely to be one of the early Melbourne clubs where they could be seen, following its opening in 1890'.[2] Against this background, Ethel Fitzpatrick's writing opens a window for us to glimpse the everyday partnership and struggle of her pioneer parents to keep food on the table and a roof over their children's heads in this same period of time:

My Father combined gardening with fishing and he used to work for E. B. White [Wight], whoever he was, and a Mr Oliver, who I know was a pastoralist, and also a certain Judge. I believe he was Judge Fellows. Anyway, Dad was working in the garden one day, digging, preparing a plot for something or other, and the Judge came out.

He watched Dad for a few minutes and then said, throwing off his coat, 'So that's the way you work, Thwaites? Well, I'll show you how to do it.' He grabbed the spade, and Father stood by and watched. The Judge tore into the work, and in a few minutes he was puffing and perspiring like a pig. In fifteen minutes, he had dug a long row and throwing down the spade and mopping his brow, he said, 'There you are, that's the way to work, my man.'

Father said, 'And now, Judge, you will go inside, have a double whisky and lay up for the rest of the day. So I'll bid you good-day, sir, and hope you will get someone more suitable than me.' And though the Judge came for my father several times, he wouldn't go. Father was very independent, knowing that he did a decent days work, always on time and he never stopped on the tick, as he called it, he never minded a few minutes here and there. He was well-respected in the community.

Another man, a Mr Beryamien, and my father, got on very well and on one occasion, he wouldn't let young Mr Beryamien in the house when his father was away. Dad always had the keys, with orders not to allow anyone access, but he was afraid he might have overstepped the mark by refusing admittance to the son. My Mother considered the son had every

right to enter the place, but Mr Beryamien commended his actions. My father had a great sense of duty and liked to feel he was trusted.

Railway Cottage

Pioneer matriarch Mary Ann Thwaites, and her daughter Ethel, were witness to the unprecedented and swift transformation of a fishing village into a smart Victorian seaside resort. In 1879, a twenty-one mile branch line was constructed from Geelong to Queenscliff at a cost of £58,000. With the new railway station being built right at her back door, the capable Mary Ann prepared meals for the railway workers. As a gesture of thanks, the Thwaites were given the leftover paint, and over the years whenever the railway maintenance crews had been through it was noticed that their house, dubbed 'Railway Cottage', soon had a fresh coat of paint the same colour as the station.

Imagine the first impressions of Victorian society women in the male-structured seaside town, with their conversations easily overheard by the founding pioneer Mary Ann Thwaites and her six daughters, living at Railway Cottage in the hub of Queenscliff, where passengers boarded and embarked from the great excursion paddle-steamers *Ozone* and *Hygeia* on one side and from the steam trains on the other. These women came from the state's capital, where Bella Guerin became the first woman to gain her degree at Melbourne University in 1883.

By 1885, there were four daily return trains running between Geelong and Queenscliff, at 7am, 12 noon, 5pm and 8pm. Across the road, ideally close to the piers and the railway station, the Esplanade Hotel was constructed in 1879. The new rail provided the heavy transport by which the gasworks could be constructed and fuelled, and the Thwaites family soon saw the transformation of the streets at night with gaslights. Close by Fishermen's Flat, The Esplanade became the fishermen's pub, with the Indigenous Australian corroborees and noisy Chinese ceremonies of the early settlement replaced by rowdy Friday night fights between the fishermen and the soldiers from the fort.

Change was in the air for Ethel, but the discontent brewing in her life was still a long way down the track. Longmire further observed that the 'New Woman', being closely related to feminism, asked for the right to self-expression, a voice in community affairs, individual fulfilment, love and social endorsement, and their own mix of feminism and femininity.

With the mature Ethel bursting to embrace these qualities of life, and the youthful Theodora joining the ranks of the feminist sisterhood, we watch, and wait to see whether the women succeed, or become trapped forever in time and place.

. . .

Our home at Fishermen's Flat was one of the first in the district. My elder brothers and sisters well remember the growth of the town of Queenscliff. The barracks, the lighthouses, piers, bridges to Swan Island, the engineers depot there, the railways — will I ever forget when the first train arrived, decorated with flags? The station and all around it gay with bunting, the band played — awful affair — but we were terribly thrilled. The first excursion paddleboat had a band on board and was gay with flags, too. The town turned out to welcome it, and we were all full of excitement and importance.

How strange it seems to look back like this. What a brief thing is life after all. I can recall so many incidents in our happy childhood. There was a creek running along at the foot of our property in which we used to bathe, for at that time bathing on the ocean beach was indictable. Think of that, the glorious ocean free to all as it should have been, was closed to us. But we owned what we called, a 'flatty'. A flat-bottomed boat in which we used to row to the middle of the creek, or the deep parts and dive in, revelling in it all. The only trouble there was the crabs. Big crabs which for some reason we called 'Scinies', and if they caught hold of your toe, and they just loved the big toe, well you'd just howl until someone released you, by putting their hand across the crab's back and pressing on its sides with little finger and thumb. They invariably let go when that happened. Years later, one of my sons caught some of the crabs and put them on the floor of the bar of the Victoria Hotel in Hesse Street and a man, who had been from one hotel to another for a drink, shot out in a panic and bolted a zigzag course up Hesse Street.

I remember the different hotels being built and the fun the children had when the workmen went home. The Grand Hotel was a lovely place in which to play. The hundreds of rooms in the building made a perfect warren of a place in which to play hide-and-seek and robbers.

There was a row of shops called Jubilee Terrace opposite our house, and a tiny house next to it where our engine driver lived before they were built. I was idly waiting for a small girl to accompany me to school and started turning over the soil with a slate pencil. It struck something hard and, uncovering it, I found a penny. Becoming enthusiastic I used my hands and found five shillings and threepence, all in coppers. Excitedly I ran home with it, and that lasted a long time to buy sweets for the three youngest of us.

...

I was always a 'broody' child. At least that was what I was called by my people. The others were always more or less active in some way, but my part in life seemed to be the onlooker. Mother declared I just sat and weighed every word and noted every look and action. If that was true when I was very young it certainly was when I grew old enough to realise my own personality, and sometimes this turning things over in my mind caused me to solve certain difficulties which from time to time presented themselves to me. In doing so, the mind seemed to use the body in this way.

I remember that upon one occasion my darning square that I had brought home from school to sew on a piece of coloured paper, both to make it look more attractive and to show up the neatness of the stitches, was mislaid. Mother and my sisters turned the house inside out looking for it. At last all hope of finding was abandoned, and even I was satisfied that it had in some way mysteriously disappeared. How disappointed I felt as I crept to bed that night. The work was a portion of the sewing that was necessary to present for the yearly examination and I did not know what to do. Exams on the morrow, the most important part missing and no earthly chance to do another piece. What was to be done?

The solution came from my sister Mary, who shared my bed. She told us in the morning, triumphantly showing us the darned work.

'Just as I was falling off to sleep,' she said, 'Ethel (myself) sat up suddenly, threw back the bed-clothes as if they were stifling her, tumbled out of bed, stood still for a second, then walked to the dressing table and carefully lifted the valance.'

It was a pretty valance of white muslin and pink sateen, under which it was gathered around the dressing table; those old dressing tables were very pretty.

'She drew out the drawer,' continued Mary, 'took the work from it, carefully replaced everything and got into bed.'

Now, the drawer mentioned was never used, except for a few things we girls treasured, to keep out of the dust and general handling, and it had not been opened for months. How did the darning get there? The family decided I must have put it there in my sleep. I do remember being worried a bit as to where I could put it to keep it safe and fresh looking, and I know from other such incidents that I must have put it there and took it out again in my sleep. I felt a bit afraid of this, but after a time got used to it: for when worried about a book which could not be found in my waking hours, I found it in my sleep.

Several times I found myself getting into bed in the middle of the night, not knowing how I got there and very frightened, too. Twice my father went out looking for me and on his return I was found sitting in the kitchen, near the empty fireplace with my nightdress and feet wet and muddy. I may have been out in the 'flatty', no-one knows. They were very good to me. Careful not to startle me, they would gently coax me to bed and for years every door was locked and the key taken away so there were no more trips abroad. If there was any more sleep walking after the age of twelve they were careful to keep it from me. As I generally felt tired in the morning after night walking, I would sometimes ask if I had been up during the night.

Mary was the watchful one, and upon my asking her if I had disturbed her she would say, 'Do you remember anything at all? Didn't you dream?'

'Nothing,' was my answer. 'But I feel tired as if I have been away somewhere.'

She thought I was taking things too seriously and it might affect my health if I brooded over it, so she began to treat it as a joke. 'Tired,' she cried. 'Well if you are, it must be at the thought of the journey you intended to take. You got out of bed in a great hurry, whilst Belle and I were talking in the next room, and we both went to your room and watched you. You were looking everywhere on the foot of the bed, on the chair, underneath the bed and then finally you sat on the bed as if concentrating on something. I said very gently, 'What are you looking for Ethel?'

And without turning your head you said, 'Stockings.'

'What do you want stockings for?'

You said, 'I want to catch a train.'

'Oh,' I said, 'you're too early. It isn't going to leave for hours and hours. Go back to bed. I'll call you in plenty of time.'

So she told me I went quietly to bed, gave a great sigh and settled down to rest again.

. . .

Several times in later years I have dreamed where I put things that were mislaid or where they have fallen. For instance, during the war I used to knit socks for the soldiers at the Front. A woman used to call for them once a week. I was a very busy woman then with seven children of my own, and all I could manage was two pairs weekly. I sat up very late the night before they were to be collected and carefully put them away, but when I came to get them, not a trace of them could be found. I had promised the socks for that day. When the woman called for them, I told her all about it. How long I had sat up to get them finished and how quietly I had moved about putting things tidy about the room and putting the finished socks together ready for pressing first thing in the morning and now, no trace of them. I could see she found it difficult to believe me, but she said that the next morning would do if sent to her before nine o'clock.

I was very worried about this and all day long was puzzling as to where they could possibly be. Toward night, however, I became very tired and sleepy and found it impossible to keep awake after being up so late the night before, and being so worried about the missing socks. Off I went to bed as early as nine o'clock and slept the sleep of the just. Suddenly I was awakened as if someone called me. I sat up wondering, then got out of bed, struck a light and found it was exactly two o'clock. Then I knew why I woke up and where to look for the socks.

Straight to the sideboard I went, opened the door and put my hand right down behind a lot of books, which were packed in it, and drew out the socks. It has remained a mystery how they got there. Either I put them in the drawer at the top and someone of the family pressed them further toward the back of the drawer so that they fell down behind it and also behind the books lower down in the sideboard itself, or I myself put them there in my sleep and in my sleep knew where they were. I cannot tell, I only know the socks were sent in before nine o'clock as requested.

My brother Jack, future Mayor of Queenscliffe

The first draft of Ethel's family memoirs referred to her brother William John as Jack when they were younger, but he seems to be later known as Bill, or Will. They had their birthdays nine days apart and he was seven years older. He married Amy Wiffen in 1890, and twenty years later, when he served his first term as Mayor of Queenscliffe, they had had ten children. From 1892 to 1897 he was a professional fisherman living on Crown Land in Beach Street, Fishermen's Flat.[3] In 1897, the year after Ethel's husband Herbert Fitzpatrick was listed as a baker renting a shop and dwelling,[4] William J. Thwaites also became a baker.[5] The following year there is no mention of him living in Fishermen's Flat. In 1910, when he became Mayor of Queenscliffe, both he and brother-in-law Herbert were well-established, each with a thriving bakery in Hesse Street.[6]

Would the Queenscliff-born William Thwaites have become Lord Mayor of the Borough of Queenscliffe and had a prominent public space, Thwaites Walk, named after him without the hand that rocked his cradle? The foundation for his public office success came from his well-educated mother, Mary Ann Thwaites, who homeschooled her elder children, first in a tent on the Queenscliff foreshore and then in their Fishermen's Flat cottage.

My second-eldest brother Jack, perhaps encouraged by the fact that Fred had come through his practical joking safely, conceived the idea of playing a joke on several Chinamen who kept a laundry. The town by then boasted several shops and the Fort had begun to be built. That meant numbers of men at work whose washing had to be catered for, hence the laundry.

This place had an ivy-covered porch with a storm lamp hanging in it. The light showed in streaks and spots through the ivy in a very uncertain way, which would make anyone standing in the shadow like a creature of one's imagination. Knowing this, Jack planned to knock at the door and step back into the shadows thrown by the ivy covering the latticed porch. He did this again and again until the Chinese were really frightened.

Then a few nights later, allowing them to become a little bolder, he stretched a line just out of the line of the light from fence to fence. Jack knocked on the door and turned to run, forgetting the line. He had planned to stoop under the line and run, thinking the Chinamen would follow and trip on the line. Instead he was caught, right across the mouth, cutting it severely in each corner, his joke turned against himself.

It wasn't uncommon for children to think up foolish and dangerous tricks, but remember in those days, fifty-six years ago, there was no sort of entertainment for young people. My elder sisters and brothers had absolutely no education, but what Mother could give them, which was only equal to about Grade Six today: to read and write well, general arithmetic, some English history. Mother had had what was then considered to be a good education for a girl in her day, which proved a boon to her family, at least the first five children.

The school was first held in a little shed-like place, at least that is the first in my memory. Being one of the younger family members, I was lucky there *was* a school, for up to that time my mother taught us English, rudimentary arithmetic and geography by maps. Our first schoolmaster was Mr Trathan, who was also organist of the Methodist Church, and his broad, rather short figure comes before me now. Benign and humourless, or was yet capable of rage at any meanness or continued flouting of authority. Many a time my brother Bill was punished for stealing apples or not doing his homework.

Bill could never resist the temptation of a certain Doctor's garden containing fruit trees, which were always laden in their season. The culprit could never be discovered until the Doctor hit upon a scheme (Bill called it a devilish scheme) to outwit the intruder. It was quite simple, to take off two palings from the fence and paint the inside edges with tar. Next morning, he went to the school, told Mr Trathan, who made all the boys hold up their hands. Needless to say what Bill's were like. The poor lad not only got a thrashing from school, but another from Father. He was always in trouble of one sort or another; those pranks were endless.

...

Nine of us were born in Victoria, and in those days of large families we helped to raise the population there. In a few years there were rows of houses, good streets, fine buildings and daily steamers bringing visitors and trips to the city by the residents.

The excursion boats of which I remember are the *Golden Crown*, the *Williams*, the *Ozone* and the last, the *Hygeia*. Many people went to see the boats off at four o'clock in the afternoon, to see and be seen. To see who had visitors and who were going away and why. And it was always a miracle to me, how some people managed to find out everything. No-one's private affairs could be kept private for long in such a small place.

As in every small town there were cliques, and to the onlooker it was great fun. If you weren't in one or other of them, you were completely out of things, I believe. There were the tradespeople, the military, the pilots, the fishermen, the engineers and so on. I remember my people telling me of the cutting out of one section from the other. I expect that has gone by the board now, but I do recollect the feud between the soldiers and the fishermen, for the former ran away with all the girls, which the latter attributed to the smart uniform and the parades with bands. There were numerous pitched battles and the soldiers' belts, with their brass buckles, were something to be reckoned with, and not a few sustained broken heads and cuts. There was never any fuss made over the result, each side wanted a fight and had it to clear the air, until another girl transferred her affections.

Australian masculinity cited as a problem to reform

While the nineteenth century Woman Movement cited Australian masculinity as a problem to reform,[7] the runaway London lovers, John and Mary Ann Thwaites, lived in harmony, raising a family of nine children and setting a fine example of shared responsibility and respect in difficult circumstances.

'Australian frontier conditions had encouraged a certain style of masculinity, which was deleterious to women and children', according to Marilyn Lake. 'His unencumbered lifestyle enabled him to indulge in distinctive leisure pursuits — casual sex, gambling, smoking and drinking deep.'[8]

There is a pattern of communities failing to acknowledge the contribution of women among the countless portraits of prominent citizens in civic buildings throughout the nation. Imagine the message this sends to the youth of today, who wonder, 'Where were the women?' Mary Ann Thwaites passed away just over a century ago, on 5 September

1913, and was rendered invisible. She died almost two years before the birth of Theodora, the youngest of her seventy grandchildren, and her Queenscliff experience was a far reach from the radical vision of equality, proposed by nineteenth century feminists:

> In order for women to become autonomous and self-determining, men would need to change their ideas about what it was to be a man; they would have to become more like the ideal woman — chaste, pure, loving, selfless, temperate, restrained, companionate.[9]

The first European men in Queenscliff were John Bowen, William Buckley and George Tobin. In 1802, Acting Lieutenant Murray, commanding the armed survey vessel *Lady Nelson*, was the first recorded entry through The Heads, with the mate John Bowen the first official white man to set foot in the Borough of Queenscliffe, very close to Bowen Road, Point Lonsdale. Between 1803 and 1835, William Buckley, an escaped convict, lived a nomadic existence with the local Indigenous people, periodically camping in a cave, which can still be seen beneath the Point Lonsdale lighthouse.

European settlement began in Queenscliff in 1838, when George Tobin read a newspaper story about countless numbers of ships lost in The Rip and saw a business opportunity. Tobin built huts on Shortland Bluff for his pilot whaleboat crews. Guiding ships through the treacherous Heads, travelling to Williamstown and swapping over, he became the first licensed Port Phillip Sea Pilot in 1839.

Queenscliff's strategic position at the entrance to Port Phillip was of significant government and military importance. Men arrived to staff the customs, health, postal, telegraph, lighthouse, signal and sea pilot's services, and they were soon followed by the military, when gold was discovered in Victoria and the defence fortifications were upgraded.

Queenscliff was already a melting pot of men in the 1860s, when wealthy gold miners moved in. By the 1880s, it was the holiday destination of the cream of Melbourne society, who built monumental private homes, hotels and guesthouses. The residents of Fishermen's Flat had a grandstand view of the busy shipping lanes into Port Phillip and the passing parade of church, political, business and intellectual identities relaxing in the place where Lt Governor La Trobe erected his family holiday home in 1844.

The finest and reputably fastest paddle-steamer ever built arrived in Queenscliff on 18 December 1886. After stopping first at Mornington and then Sorrento on her maiden voyage, the *Ozone*, with two paddle wheels, a dark green hull with white upper sections and two orange funnels, like a big boy's toy, famously collided with the Queencliff Pier while racing the clock. Baillieu House immediately changed the hotel's name to the more fashionable 'Ozone', after the three-decked paddle-steamer that had electric lighting only seven years after Thomas Edison marketed this invention to the world, as well as a ladies hair salon, a luxurious dining room and various bars.[10] In 1890, an even more glamorous and faster paddle-steamer, the *Hygeia*, joined *Ozone* to meet the demands of the 'Health and Pleasure Trips on Port Phillip Bay'.[11]

Chapter 3

Ethel

Silencing Fish Wives — women can't sing, paint, write or think

On Friday evening of 19 March 2010, I joined the audience at the Boatshed of the Queenscliffe Maritime Museum, for the annual recital of 'Fishy Tales'. Attracted by the theme 'The Last of the Lifeboat Men', appropriately in a building on reclaimed land in Wharf Street where the old Fisherman's Wharf once stood and near where Ethel was born, I sat taking notes.

We were reminded that the event was called 'Fish Wives Tales' in 2009, and I was immediately disappointed to have missed a research opportunity. A DVD was available, the president told us, but due to a technical hitch the sound was missing. The women's narratives had been lost and the audience thought it was a huge joke.

Was someone being intentionally evasive here? Exactly who was colluding to hide the feminine side of the Borough of Queenscliffe? The answer is probably: nobody and everybody. The 2010 winter edition of *Meanjin* offered a timely look at the continuing exclusion of women in Australia, supported by the following statistics, mentioned in a newspaper review:

> Australia Post released its Australian Legends of the Written Word stamp series, Ms Cunningham observes. Five men, one woman — novelist Colleen McCullough.
>
> Only three of the 34 finalists of the Archibald Prize for 2010 were women. And last year, not a single female lead singer was included in Triple J's Hottest 100 survey.

'I could go on,' says Cunningham, 'I won't.'

'I'll just say this: either women can't sing, paint, write or think as well as they used to … or we live in a culture that does not like the things women say, or does not know how to hear them when they say it.'[1]

Women's equal right to vote alongside men

Ethel was sixteen in 1891, when women's demands for women's suffrage gathered force with the collection of over 30,000 Victorian women's signatures in a 'Monster Petition', calling for women's equal right to vote alongside men in the State Parliament elections. It is significant that the Shire of Queenscliffe recorded only a single signatory,[2] compared to 119 from the Shire of Colac from a population of 7000.[3] What was the reason for the silence of the women of Queenscliff?

By matching a clue from Ethel Fitzpatrick's family memoirs — the reason why her Church of England mother was unwelcome at Queenscliff's St George the Martyr, Church of England, with findings that when women signed the petition in the pastoral west at Casterton the community was divided along class lines[4] — a picture emerges:

> Mary Gilmore, who lived in Casterton during this period, wrote that no-one could have friendship with the lower orders. They were as far removed from the equalities of friendship as Negro slaves. The women talked to each other as if from a distance. This description suggests that class loyalties were more important than gender. Class divisions may have prevented women from uniting to advocate for women's suffrage.[5]

The ability of Queenscliff women to organise suffrage activities was doubtful with the prevalent class separation and, as voiced by a woman who wrote to the *Colac Herald*, 'some poor women are too timid to even suggest' the franchise be extended to them 'in the presence of male relatives, for it is easy to sneer at a woman's progress.'[6]

Ethel the observant churchgoer

The first church of the Queenscliff Wesleyan congregation, which included the Thwaites family, was built in 1868, on the corner of Hesse and Stokes Streets. This small grey sandstone building where Ethel Thwaites attended Sunday School, is now a bookshop, almost unchanged from the times described by Ethel in her journals:

The Churches were a gathering place every Sunday. Queenscliff was a garrison town and there were Church parades headed by a military band with a drum major twirling his staff, which was decorated with a gilt globe and crown on the top. To me, he was fascinating. Straight as a die, precise step, a gorgeous figure — the way he managed that staff, round his head and round and round in his hand with never a look to the right or left, he had the army following him like a lamb.

My Mother rejoiced in the increasing amenities and loved the open spaces, sunshine, great expanse of sky, particularly the latter at night, to see so many stars and the great moon in the autumn. The Church which she had missed so much, the lovely Church of England which she was brought up to attend, was not comforting to her. It was attended by splendidly dressed men and women, who being of ample means were attracted to the little seaside town, and she found herself brushed out of the way by these people and coldly received by the verger and church authorities. So she took her family to the little non-conformist church where there was always a welcome. For years she missed the Church of England form of services. There were no responses and no participation excepting in the hymns. But she got used to it in time and actually disliked the English service as 'man made', which seems rather strange to me now.

Thinking of the Church reminds me of the different characters who attended. One sweet old lady dressed in black frocks nearly to the ground, with faded looks and wrinkled skin, had such a sweet, patient expression. I have never seen anyone like her since and I have often thought what a wonderful study she was for an artist. Her prayers were a model of humility and holiness. I was a very critical child, but she disarmed all criticism with her sweetness, lovely manners and voice.

. . .

One of my sisters, Mary, was a great mimic and could draw a little, enough for the victim to be identified. Many a time in Church when we were weary beyond words of the long drawn-out sermons and prayers, she would pass around a caricature of the minister or any member of the congregation that struck her fancy at the time. There were many arresting, amusing and odd characters in those far-off days, and we got a great deal of fun out of them.

I was made to attend the weekly prayer meetings, which I very much resented, and to interest and amuse myself, took stock of the participants. A Mr and Mrs Peter Angel I was most intrigued with. He always began his prayers with the words, 'I tang de Lord,' followed by a long list of the things he was thankful for. His wife had the Bible Class at Sunday School. I used to be enthralled with her, so ugly, yet so kindly. Her lower teeth came outward over the upper teeth and were big and yellow. She knew her Bible like the back of her hand and would fire a question at you, pointing with a finger covered with a black glove turning up at the end — she always wore black gloves, ever so much too big — and woe betide you if your thoughts had been wandering.

Sometimes I was so interested in her face and teeth that for a second I did not realise she was addressing me. Then she would cover me with a scornful look.

'*You*. You whom I have tried to teach the Word of God, letting your mind wander on worldly matters. Do you mean to say you didn't *hear* my question?'

Then one would humbly beg her pardon and ask for the question to be repeated. Once I remember she asked what I knew of St Paul's conversion. That was quite a question from that lady, for it meant you were to take ten minutes or so of the lesson time telling of his life before his conversion, where it occurred, and the effect it had on his life afterwards. She made you feel disgraced if you didn't know, as she put it, after all the work for your benefit.

An old fisherman I remember who rejoiced in the name of Van Leen, said he was a Russian Finn. He wore gold earrings and had a bushy beard and long hair; he looked like a pirate, but was as mild as a lamb. He had a slow, quiet way of speaking, although I could never understand a word he said. An Italian who, for some reason I could never explain, reminded me of Garibaldi, had a voice deep as the bass note of an organ when he sang. I loved to hear him in church. We never knew his name. He landed from a big ship anchored way offshore and only came in to go to church.

The churches were filled in those days. Fathers with their wives and numerous families filled the long pews. There was great excitement on Harvest Festivals and Sunday School Anniversaries, and a picnic was a great affair. The whole town turned out en force, with buses always gay with flags and waving and cheering children. Now they wouldn't give tuppence for a picnic of that sort, or if they would it would only be tiny children.

. . .

I dimly remember a place, which could hardly be called a room; it was more like a store shed with broken windows, dirt floor and benches. For my life I cannot recall the teacher and I am very hazy about the new brick school. But I do distinctly recollect a man with a benevolent expression and a determined stride who took charge of the new school. He played the organ and led the singing in the little church where Father, Mother and the whole family attended. I loved the school and had no difficulty to assimilate the very meagre curriculum.

It was because of this man that I became fond of music. It was always a source of real trouble to him that the majority of children seemed quite indifferent to melody. The facilities of course were practically nil, and he had an uphill struggle in teaching them the beautiful English folk songs, so familiar to me. When we hear them over the air, I often wish it had been possible for my mother to have done so. My father's people were

musical and his brother, my Uncle Geoffrey, was an organist in a cathedral in London.

Father was so glad to see the love of music was to live again. He bought an organ for me and on this, without any tuition and with the aid of books alone, I tried to emulate the schoolmaster's example. By doing so I was led to love only the best, and by mastering some easy settings of the masters by teachers and others I became efficient enough to play in the Church and Sunday School at sixteen years of age. Naturally I was by no means wonderful, yet was able to play nearly all of the accompaniments to the singers who were visitors to Queenscliff when it was called 'Queen of Watering Places'. Also to play for visiting choirs of which there were quite a few during the summer months. By the time singers and choirs came from the cities, childhood was well past.

The traditions that link women together

Ethel's diary invites connections with the Thwaites women and the traditions that link women together at the beginning of the twentieth century. Not only does the life story of the Australian composer Margaret Sutherland, born in 1897, serve to place the patriarchal experiences of Ethel in the context of those of privileged academic women, Sutherland emerges as a guiding light and a heroine for women and girls today.

In Anne Longmire's *The Catalysts: Change and Continuity 1910–2010*, we find the gentle, dignified Sutherland disparaged personally and professionally by some who regarded composing as solely a male preserve. How bad could that be for a woman from the top drawer of society? Two lines written by Longmire must tug at the heartstrings of anyone who has ever nurtured the hopes and dreams of tender young people of either gender: 'Sutherland played a vital role in the development of musical composition in Australia. In pursuing her tough quest, early family encouragement became a comforting later memory.'[7]

Sutherland and Fitzpatrick were raised in a patriarchal society that programmed talented girls to lose their way in motherhood. In an ideal world, their education would have included a balanced historical record of the lives of successful and artistic women. However, such a book had not been written, and not much has changed in the twenty-first century. Today, when women return from fulfilling their 'biological destiny' of birthing, mothering and housekeeping to resume their careers, there is often no fanfare, acclaim or recognition, though there should be.

> Sutherland had moved into a selfish and abusive territory when she married Norman Albiston, a clinical psychologist, in 1926. He scoffed at her work, bemoaned her lack of domesticity, questioned her mental fitness in pursuing both music and motherhood, demanded she stay home and tend to their two children for he had a career to pursue and thought her mad. They divorced in 1948. The conflict was damaging, for Sutherland was being forced to relinquish her desire to compose and had come face to face with patriarchy, which cast her into the contradictory role of a culture-preserver as a mother and a culture threat in audaciously lining up as a female composer.[8]

Over and over again, we fail to conceptualise the unique female destiny and to prepare both our female offspring and our corporate structures to expect interrupted, but fabulous, career paths combined with motherhood. When 'Fish Wives Tales' were joked about at 'Fishy Tales', it had the appearance of popular approval that women's voices were yet again suppressed and lost from the history of Queenscliff. Women still have to fall back on 'comforting memories' when, like Sutherland, they find themselves in an intolerable place.

Chapter 4
Ethel
Tyranny and humiliation in Fitzpatrick's Bakery

On 29 November 1893, eighteen-year-old Ethel Thwaites married baker Herbert Fitzpatrick. He was born in Carlton and his parents are shown as 'unknown' in a Queenscliff Museum, Fishermen's Flat, research document.[1]

Herbert and Ethel Fitzpatrick lived, ran a business and raised their family two doors from the Victoria Hotel in Hesse Street, Queenscliff, between 1896 and 1919. Their family of seven children included three girls and four boys, with Mavis and Harold deceased. In order of birth they were Dulcie, Herbert, Mabel (Mavis), James (Harold), Geoffrey, Edgar (Bill) and Theodora, the youngest, who was also the youngest of the seventy grandchildren of Queenscliff pioneers John and Mary Ann Thwaites.

The Victoria Hotel had been trading since 1871. A modest establishment catering for around thirty guests until the 1950s, it was promoted as 'two minutes from the main beach and pier' and it boasted 'an excellent table'.[2] It was a prime location for the bakery, but Ethel struggled to raise a young family and maintain a thriving business.

Farmer's widow opens tearooms

Ethel never forgot the tyranny and humiliation dished out to her as a teenage bride, a new mother and fulltime shop assistant, living and raising children on the Hesse Street bakery premises. However, the observant Ethel, who'd recorded the details of the Wesleyan Church congregation of the late 1800s, remembered and wrote a firsthand account of how it was for the women around her in the early 1900s.

Working in her husband's Queenscliff business, Ethel recorded the attempts of a widow to make a fresh start in the resort town. Her observations provide significant data that early Queenscliff was a progressive and feminism-friendly place, with opportunities for women to start their own businesses that didn't exist elsewhere:

I remember a woman coming to Queenscliff with her two children, and opening a fruit and lolly shop and tearooms. She had lost her husband who was a farmer, and knowing she couldn't carry on the farm, which was mortgaged, she had sold it. With the amount left she came to try to get a living in that way. After paying rent and the fact that trade was practically nil in the winter, she tried a boarding house business. Not being able to put up a sufficient amount of money for a decent house, the best she could do was rent an old place, and take workingmen and a few casuals for meals. Her little daughter, only sixteen years old, kept the shop going with the assistance of an aunt in the summer.

In the boarding house, one of the lodgers became ill and the Doctor pronounced it to be typhoid fever. Mrs Mentiplay nursed him through the whole sickness, of course having to close the house for business, which was a big strain on her resources, but she did carry it through and the grateful sick man proposed marriage to her. Mr Brownlow would not listen to her protests about difference in age and her poor circumstances (she was ten years older than he) and they announced their plans to her children.

The daughter, Olive, was terribly upset and begged her mother to give up the idea of remarriage and, consequently, so worried was the child that she contracted meningitis in a very bad form, and in her delirium babbled about her mother's desertion of her family and that never again would they be all in all to one another. The child died and now the shop was closed, and the mother felt she couldn't go through with the marriage. After some months passed, Mr Brownlow succeeded in persuading her to alter her mind and the marriage went forward.

. . .

I was flabbergasted one morning when Mrs Mentiplay called and asked me to play for the wedding in the Church. That was alright, but what upset me was the fact that she intended getting married in the traditional white with long veil and orange blossom. I mildly remonstrated, but she was positive about the plans.

'I was married to my first husband in Salvation Army uniform, with no veil or flowers or any of the lovely fittings of a bride, and now I don't give two hoots what anybody says. They can even laugh if they want to, but I'm going to be a real bride this time.'

I remember people did laugh and the church was crowded to see the fun, as they called it.

Well, it seemed that poor Olive, the daughter, had some premonition of trouble ahead, for they went to Sydney for the honeymoon and whilst there, Mr Brownlow obtained a position permanently. They were married about six months when I received a letter from him with the news that they were crossing the road one night, when they were struck by a motor-fiend and both knocked unconscious. Mr Brownlow recovered after a few hours in hospital, but his wife had suffered frightful injuries to her leg, which resulted in amputation, and later her death. His letter was a rather heart-rending epistle in which he blamed himself for insisting on ignoring Olive's pleading not to marry. He couldn't forgive himself, although he knew that for the short time together she was happier than she had ever been, and was so glad her son had someone to look after his welfare. His own words were, 'Nemesis struck sudden and hard. It was a bolt out of the blue.'

Local lass jilted by married soldier

In 1921, Louisa Lawson made the first public women's suffrage speech in New South Wales, campaigning for women's rights, especially the right to vote and change relations between men and women with the ballot. She observed matter-of-factly: 'Here in Australia, it is considered more a crime to steal a horse than to ruin a girl.' Three years earlier, Lawson established a journal, *Dawn*, as a mouthpiece for Australian women.[3] All this was happening around the time a young Queenscliff woman was jilted by a married soldier, which was mentioned by Ethel:

As the children grew up, love and courtship and sometimes tragedy came to us there. I remember one case of a girl and a young soldier. In fact, as I have said, there seemed to be very little going on that was not as open as the day. Everybody knew everything that was happening, and we watched and waited for what we considered to be the inevitable marriage. But that did not occur, for what we noticed next was the absence of the soldier and Mary M's illness. She was a very sick girl and the Doctor pronounced that she had no malady that he could cure. It eventually transpired that the soldier was already married — a great shock to the girl, who of course immediately became ill.

When she recovered she was a different creature: quiet and uninterested in all the activities going on. Then she too disappeared, and her relatives were in the dark as to where she had gone and quite naturally were most concerned. After some weeks her mother received a cablegram telling of her arrival in Cape Town. There was a wave of intense excitement over the village. All that way off and she only twenty-three! What would happen to her? Had she gone off with the young wretch who had caused her so much unhappiness? Conjecture and more conjecture. A few months passed, and then more news. Mary had been advised to open a boarding house — small at first — where the labour was cheap and the returns very good indeed from the white people, both visitors and workers who were in need of such a service.

Many years after, when Mary returned for a visit to the old home, she was a rich woman. She told me she hadn't to lift a finger; the boys who worked for her did everything for almost nothing. They were clean and honest and most efficient, doing her slightest bidding, and she often felt sorry for the black boys that she couldn't offer them more. She had been warned not to do so, or she would be overwhelmed with many more wanting to work for her. But she could and did feed them well, and often gave them clothes, which she had bought especially for them, telling them they were given to her to dispose of by people leaving South Africa.

Fitzpatrick's Bakeries and Excessive Workload for Ethel

From 1901 to 1908, Herbert operated a second business on land he owned in Point Lonsdale, while he rented the Hesse Street bakery from W. S. Jamieson of 'Glamis', Gellibrand Street.[4] The 1909 shire rate records indicate additions to the shop and dwelling in Hesse Street, and without mention of Jamieson as the property owner after 1904 one must surmise that around this time, or following the sale of the shop and land in Point Lonsdale, Herbert purchased and made improvements to the Hesse Street bakery, which he owned until 1948.

Fitzpatrick's Bakery had a narrow frontage. Talking to Jack Beazley, a local boat builder born in 1929, I got a detailed description of the premises in the thirties and forties, when baker Alex Ahearn rented it from Herbert Fitzpatrick. Jack remembered that there was a boarding house with a green trellis between the bakery and the Victoria Hotel, and on the other side there was a tennis court next to the driveway to the Whitehall Guest House. 'The bakery was twenty-five feet by fifteen feet,' he said, 'with a large glass window and a glass counter over the cakes. The door behind the counter led to the residence, with a side gate on the right opening to some steep stairs, which were difficult with the bakery below.'

Raising their eldest children, Dulcie, Herbert, Mavis and Harold, in what she described as the unhealthy environment of a bakery, cake and sweets shop, Ethel mentions constant criticism from all quarters, and hints darkly in her 1940s diaries that some men have a lot to answer for. Women's excessive workload was a feminist issue for decades:

> … the plight of the 'working mother' has long been a cause of feminist concern in Australia and it remains so. It was the

> socialist friend of women, writer and organiser William Lane, who named women 'the weary sex' in his late nineteenth century novel *The Workingman's Paradise*, and labour women's organiser Lilian Locke-Burns who coined the slogan 'One Woman One Job' in the support of the campaign for motherhood endowment in the 1920s.[5]

In the paper, 'The Economic Independence of the Married Woman', delivered by suffragist Rose Scott in 1903, she sought to alter the position of wife, from degraded sexual slave to self-governing partner.[6] Ethel recollects in her 1940s diaries, 'I was being goaded into work, in pregnancy, in nursing young babies and trying to bear the burden of catering for food and clothes for a family on a pittance, and being censored and bullied for not being able to do so.'

Feminists who followed in her path argued for the economic independence of married women in their capacity as the mothers of the nation, as citizens and workers. As mothers, women were the hardest of hard workers, always on call, 'always ready to manage, nurse and attend to the numerous wants of those who are constantly appealing to her'. As mothers of future citizens, women performed work of vital civic importance: they ought not be forced to neglect this vital role in order to earn economic independence in the labour market. The mother had 'a right to an independent position in the home'. Whereas Scott argued that legislation should entitle the wife to a share of the husband's income, her successors, influenced by Labor and socialist ideas circulating in Britain, began to advocate a scheme of motherhood endowment, an income paid by the state to women in their capacity as workers and citizens.[7]

Like her mother before her, Ethel had her last baby in her forties, but when the third and fourth of her seven children died, aged fifteen and eighteen, it must have seemed that their family was split in half forever. Ethel and Herbert buried two children while they were still only teenagers: James Harold (1904–19) and Mabel Mavis (1902–20). Their death certificates reveal that Harold died of acute rheumatism and heart disease that he had suffered from the age of eight. The following year, the tragedy was compounded with the unexpected death of eighteen-year-old Mavis from lymphatic leukaemia and respiratory failure, after being ill for only a fortnight.

Loss and grief

All the Fitzpatrick women: Ethel, Dulcie and Theodora, suffered from the death of Mavis. On the surface Ethel and Dulcie got on with life, but privately they endured three decades of torment, which took their toll on the fabric of family life. Theo moved away to conquer the Tasmanian wilderness, while her mother and sister struggled in an emotional wilderness. When Theo cut loose from her mother, the finality was a long time dawning on Ethel. There is a cruel edge to the Tasmanian correspondence between mother and daughter, which has one alternating between sympathy, frustration and despair for them both.

The Fitzpatricks' eldest child, Dulcie, was twenty when Theo was born in 1915. Dulcie married and had two sons. Winston was born in 1919, the year Dulcie's brother Harold died. John was born on her birthday, about two months after the unexpected death of her sister Mavis, on 9 December 1920.

With the birth of both grandchildren overshadowed by the deaths of two of her children, Ethel spent the next part of her life wholeheartedly focused on getting it right for the three younger Fitzpatricks after the difficult years of raising the four older children on a business premises. One can guess that Dulcie's sadness was sharpened by a sense of loss when her family moved from Queenscliff to the Mannerim farm, and she saw her mother fully satisfied while she nurtured Geoffrey, Bill and Theo, with Theo in particular close in age to her children.

Ethel wrote 'Recuperating in the country', a complex story about the healing process of the Fitzpatrick family. This ambitious piece of elegiac prose is the writing of a mother who mourned the loss of a son and a daughter who were on the threshold of adulthood. Her son, weakened by an early childhood illness, had lived for many years with the relative who was mentioned on his death certificate. It is therefore understandable that the story is centred on the memory of her daughter, Mavis, whose death at eighteen was sudden and unexpected. This was the same age at which Ethel married, with the same minister, the Reverend John Adams, officiating at both her marriage and her daughter's funeral.

Destitute doctor's wife finds work as the Koroit postmistress in 1878

When dark-haired Ethel Richardson, destined to become writer Henry Handel Richardson, lived in Queenscliff late in 1877, Ethel Thwaites was a two-and-a-half year old. Ethel Richardson detested her name as a child and preferred to be called Ettie.[8] With her parents and blonde younger sister Lil, Ettie had recently returned from a grand tour of Europe, which was curtailed by the collapse of her wealthy father's mining share portfolio and the necessity for him to return to a general medical practice for a living. Her mother Mary kept up genteel appearances, with Ettie and Lil seen about town wearing white frocks starched stiff as cardboard,[9] black stockings and boaters.

Ettie, the doctor's daughter, lived in a house on the hill, at 26 Mercer Street, a world away from Ethel the fisherman's daughter growing up in humble Wharf Street. Destined to become an internationally acclaimed writer, she attended primary school in Queenscliff with Ethel's brother, William Thwaites, the future five-time Mayor of Queenscliffe.

Dr Richardson had sought an easy government job as a quarantine officer at Queenscliff, when he was unable to maintain successive general practices in Hawthorn and Chiltern due to the onset of symptoms associated with syphilis, contracted decades earlier when he was a medical student in Edinburgh. However, the only way to check the crews and passengers of sailing ships for disease, as is still the case with present-day Port Phillip Sea Pilots taking ships through The Heads, was to climb a ladder on the side of a vessel, often pitching dangerously in the ocean swell.

Ethel writes that her brother Bill was partial to an unnamed doctor's apples. There is an early photo of a pre-1860 timber building built for Dr Alexander Philadelphia Lamb Robertson, one of the earliest medical officers stationed in Queenscliff. It is probably Robertson pictured in the gig in front of the house. His assistant health officer and later his successor, Dr David John Williams, built the simpler adjoining structure before 1863 and this still stands, now minus the veranda. Dr Williams later leased his house to a relieving medical officer, Dr Richardson.[10]

Walter Richardson was appointed to the post of Acting Health Officer and, from early 1878, also to that of Acting Tide Surveyor, positions previously held by Dr Williams. It was obvious to all and sundry that the new doctor struggled physically with these tasks. As his health steadily declined, people assumed incorrectly that his delusions and memory loss were alcohol related. There was public humiliation for Ettie Richardson, frequently summoned to Hesse Street when her father forgot where he lived.[11] In June 1878, with the deterioration of his mental health, he was relieved of these positions and subsequently admitted to Cremorne Private Hospital in Richmond on 11 September 1878, leaving his family destitute in Queenscliff.[12]

In *Ultima Thule*, Ethel Richardson (as Henry Handel) writes:

'By God! What's to become of us?'

...

> Boarders were out of the question: for Richard's sake. What could she do? What did other women do who were left in her plight, with little children dependant on them? Driving her mind back she saw that as a rule these 'widows and things' were content to live at somebody else's expense, to become the limpets known as 'poor relations', leaving the education of their children to a male relative.
>
> . . .
>
> 'It's not money I want this time, Tilly,' she wrote: and Tilly was but one of the many who, the news of Richard's breakdown having spread abroad as on an invisible telegraph, came forward with offers of help. 'It's work. I don't care what; if only I can earn enough to keep us together.' But here even Tilly's ingenuity failed her: women of Mary's standing (let alone her advanced age, her inexperience) did not turn out of their sheltered homes and come to grips with the world.[13]

Mary Richardson's situation, going from being a Queenscliff doctor's wife to a postmistress at Koroit, highlights both the hardship and heroism of Australian frontier women. The published letters of Dr Walter Richardson when he was testing the waters to set up a medical practice in Queenscliff and the employment records of William Thwaites, preserved in the Queenscliffe Council Rate Books, both serve to showcase the challenges for men supporting a family in the fishing village, and point to the enormity of the task for a woman alone to make ends meet.

The two Queenscliff Ethels, strangers as children, both with literary and musical leanings, both destined to write about the Queenscliff of the 1880s, almost certainly met as adults. The written recollections of Ethel Fitzpatrick leave an indelible handprint, illuminating the courageous lives of the pioneer women of Queenscliff. The revelation of a published author approaching Ethel for material for her next book becomes secondary to the windows she has provided into the experience and contribution of women in the early days with her firsthand accounts of her mother, the fisherman's wife; Mrs Peter Angel, also a fisherman's wife; the farmer's widow, Mrs Mentiplay; and the jilted soldier's fiancée, Mary M.

Queenscliff was the seventh childhood home of writer Henry Handel Richardson, who referred to it as 'a little watering-place on the Bay'.[14] She wrote, 'my love of the sea and everything to do with it has amounted to a passion.'[15]

Ethel Thwaites also wrote a beautiful description of Shortlands Bay, in Chapter Seven of her novella *Upheaval*: 'Standing on the veranda, facing south and looking towards the sea, Mary could see the sand hills outlining the Straits. Before the war she often stood there watching the white sails of the fishing boats moving about like white butterflies over the blue sea.'

Henry Handel Richardson subsequently wrote in *Myself When Young*, which was published in 1948 after her death, 'Like most up-country townships Maldon contained a number of oddities, or at least people unusual enough to strike a "noticing child".'[16] In this regard, the two young Ethels were like a pair of gloves, for it seems that this observation was equally true of Queenscliff and young Ethel Thwaites, who remembered and wrote some astonishing details of the congregation of the small grey sandstone Wesleyan Church on the corner of Stokes and Hesse Streets.

That Ethel Thwaites and Ettie Richardson, for one moment in time, were so tantalisingly close that they transferred some shared experiences is more than idle conjecture. Thwaites Walk, in Queenscliff, might have been named after all the Thwaites men, but it is not beyond the realm of possibility that the Thwaites women may be present in the literature of Henry Handel Richardson. The following line, to give a further example, could be either of their mothers speaking: '... she hotly declared that there wasn't a child of our age fit to associate with. Now that we had come down in the world she went, I suppose, in fear of our picking up common ways of speech or losing our manners.'[17]

When we were all married, some of us stayed in Queenscliff going into business for ourselves. As the town grew, there was great competition among the tradespeople to get the custom of newcomers and visitors, especially in the summertime, when the excursion steamers and trains arrived. The tradespeople lined up at the barriers with printed cards denoting their trade and soliciting custom. It must have been a tremendous nuisance to people, impeding their way and I'm sure the most importunate never got the trade they were so anxious for.

We loved meeting the different types of residents and visitors, some of whom were most interesting. One old lady used to come to the shop for a few buns for herself and 'Willie', her husband. He was as silent as she was voluble. She would hold us up for half-an-hour or so to recant the symptoms of bronchitis, pneumonia or 'fulerfelossis'. We were some time finding out that the latter meant tuberculosis.

One visitor to the town was an authoress, travelling for material for her next book. I have forgotten her name, but I remember she asked me endless questions about the growth of Queenscliff. I did wish then that I had been more heedful of what my parents had often talked about. Not being allowed to mix with other children because of their careless speech, we girls found an outlet in reading and the world of imagination.

It is entirely possible that Ethel's memorable interview with an authoress was with Henry Handel Richardson, when she came to Australia in 1912 to research *The Fortunes of Richard Mahony*.[18] Ethel's second-youngest child, Bill, would have been two years old, and one imagines the pair arranging to meet away from children, customers and the busy Fitzpatrick's bakery, cake and sweets shop.

Chapter 5
Theo
Adolescence on the Bellarine Peninsula

Theodora Ethel Fitzpatrick was born at Queenscliff on 20 December 1915. Her father's business, H. A. Fitzpatrick's Bakery, was advertised in the local paper from 1896 until 1919.[1] As well, in 1901 Herbert opened Point Lonsdale's first shop on the corner of Point Lonsdale Road and The Esplanade (now 4 Ocean Road), opposite the lighthouse reserve and south of Dunk's Coffee Palace, selling newspapers, sweets, jam and tinned salmon, until he sold the business around 1908.[2] Around 1923 he leased their Hesse Street shop, bakery and dwelling to baker Richard Wibley,[3] bought a farm in nearby Mannerim, whereupon Herbert and Ethel retired to unaccustomed rural life.

The adolescent Theo, the youngest child of Ethel and Herbert, wrote a vibrant account of her family life in the aftermath of a house fire in which they lost their home and all their possessions. The surviving writing by the mother and daughter is post Mannerim house fire. In 'The Story of Liebchen', we find the adolescent Theo brimming with natural curiosity and imagination, writing the first words of *herstory*, on the threshold of a future that will unfold in a biography about three generations of her family. Feminist writer Melissa Benn, herself the mother of two girls, defined adolescence in *What Should We tell Our Daughters, The Pleasures and Pressures of Growing Up Female*, and her definition becomes the stage where we pick up Theo's story:

> Adolescence is, by definition, the process of slow managed separation of parent and child. At the same time, all parents, because they were once children, understand the lasting impact

> we are likely to have on our offspring, the many ways that our words — and more hauntingly — our deeds live long within our children's lives, for good or ill.[4]

'The Story of Liebchen'

We read 'The Story of Liebchen', wondering what the future holds for the impressionable Theo Fitzpatrick, writing in the late 1920s, growing up in the isolation of the Bellarine Peninsula, with the seaside resort of Queenscliff on the horizon and Geelong tucked away in the distance.

She came to us in a cane shopping basket: a little yellow-grey fluffy kitten with great, wide, speaking eyes, forlorn, far from home and hungry. Our home had been burnt to the ground, but on its ashes we were building another and so far we four were scattered in different homes about the countryside, except my brother who lived in the big barn for the time, to take care of the farm at night and to build the new house.

We were poorer and wiser for this experience and one of our new interests was this little morsel of a kitten, which shrank from us all. Richard Tauber was singing 'Liebchen, mein Liebchen' from every station on the radio, so we gave her her first drink of warm milk and christened her Liebchen.

Her first day was spent in shy observance of us all; an intent stocktaking of my father, greyer and more stooped since the day of the fire; my mother, with her plump motherly figure, and frequent intervals of gazing blankly while her thoughts ranged far away; my black-eyed brother, always up at the crack of dawn and whistling most of the day; and myself, as broad as long, preparing to take an examination two months ahead, with my books all gone.

Liebchen studied us from afar and kept her thoughts to herself, and it was several days before she consented to play among the floor joists, with tentative pats at blocks of wood hundreds of times her size. When visitors arrived she froze into quietness, and accepted our protection without the slightest sign of acknowledging any obligation.

...

Liebchen became as much part of the house as the very walls that rose up under my brother's skilful fingers. She spent her day in splendid freedom, often having a game amongst the timbers destined to be our home, or accompanying me down the orchard, where a rug beneath the trees and in the long grasses was a delightful place to study. The kitten was a welcome diversion from the dreary couplets of Pope and the labour of translation. Sprawling panting over reference books, she often chose Bradley's 'Shakespeare' as a little platform upon which she cleaned the faintest trace of dust from her lissom body. It was from these early jaunts that Liebchen learned her lifelong dislike of minahs, which are the bush policemen: for such small birds, their voice is amazingly harsh and shrill. They tormented her, swooping low with an energetic playfulness, but not low enough to be caught.

It was while my brother still used the barn, a big sweet-smelling place stocked with grain, that Liebchen became familiar with it and made it her castle. First it was near the cowsheds, and to a kitten with her lust for milk, that was one remove from Paradise; and it was near the haystacks, where you only had to tread lightly and wait a few minutes before you heard the tantalising sounds of rats and mice. This was the most fascinating place to Liebchen, who sat with the patience of a scientist, thinking inscrutable thoughts, and only needing the nose of a mouse to appear to have that morsel for her tea.

When much older, Liebchen sat near the stack or in the barn, meditating for long hours before the victim appeared. Whether these rats had formed a suicide club, or whether they knew she'd have them in the long run and gave up in despair to walk into her sharp white claws, our puss did not go hungry for her own meal. Ours she never accepted, but she knew the hour when the buckets of milk came clanking down the track, and never missed her enormous saucers of milk.

Most cats put their noses into this and never lift their heads for air, but Liebchen drank with three laps and a really stupendous gulp with quite monotonous regularity. After the drink came a cleaning up schedule, religiously observed, and a sunning if it were morning, or in the evening a dignified retreat into the chaff-cutter house where a cat may sleep on the fine cut hay, and be comfortable and very clean.

Have you ever smelt wormwood when the mists of the morning have cleared away? Or the sweet smell of hay when the dew is freshly on it? Or the delicate scent of briar in the evening? And mint, when a southern wind is blowing? Our Liebchen came up for her milk every morning, and evidently had spent the night in any one of these vicinities, for we caught the smell of the lingering sweetness in her long fur.

My brother and I have magic we use with cats — a high falsetto, which is crammed full of intense love for animals, and they know it; a soft spoken word for dogs; a confidential voice for horses; a whistle on one note for ducks and just the right intonation for cows when you rub between the horns or around the neck. A high falsetto steals all resistance from cats and they stop in mid-flight: it is only a fragment of the magic the Pied Piper used, but quite the same sort.

We used to bribe Liebchen to sit on our knees with whispered caresses whilst she shut her eyes and looked like a lovely little witch cat, with white wisps sticking out her ears, long sensitive whiskers and long antennae of eyelashes. We would tell her hers was the face that launched a thousand ships and that half our kingdom was hers. If she stayed on our knees we would tell her where there was a bumptious big rat simply asking to have the starch taken out of him, or taught an everlasting lesson by no-one but the cleverest cat ever invented.

'Simpering little devil,' Father would mutter. Father treated her with respect, but petted all the other cats to make up for our lack of attention to them. But Father and Liebchen were quite polite to each other, because Liebchen was a splendid ratter in the stacks and then, of course, Father usually brought in the milk buckets.

. . .

It was about two years after her arrival that our beloved cat developed the habit of taking her midnight catches of particularly succulent rats into my brother's sleep-out and putting them right under his nose as he slept. We used to hear the most lurid language on these occasions, but of course the culprit was never bludgeoned because he understood her point of view: if my brother could always treat her so well, surely he would relish delicacies that had to be caught with infinite patience and skill.

She loved our big country fires, and never failed to monopolise the footstool at nights to dream away the hot hours in luxurious relaxation. There was even one night when, half-melted, she actually fell off the footstool onto the rug, and sat there dazedly for several minutes, unable to comprehend the full significance of her downfall. On nights when the radio music filled the room loudly with the unearthly music of the masters, she nestled more snugly down, and purred her gentle, almost inaudible applause.

Gentleness was one facet of her character and another was that she so strongly resented visitors that she fled the house if anyone strange arrived, with the exception of callers like the butcher or baker, who rattled up the drive with their high-stepping, brisk horses. With the minahs making a great noise and the dog barking at these intruders, Liebchen became frenzied, running from window to window, growling fiercely, her eyes enormous, yellow and vicious, and her Persian tail five times its usual size.

She had one habit that revolted me more than anything did. On fine summer evenings, we lit the lamps and left the windows open, no blinds were drawn and moths arrived — big, stupid moths, trying to reach the flame or the bright reflection in the glass. How could they know that a cat, with the yellow of her eyes half-hidden by the dilated black pupils, sat inside the curtains, unerringly dealing with all intruders into our place? Moths fluttering about would have been heaven compared with the businesslike and sickening crunches they made in Liebie's jaws.

The country has lovely quiet changes that accompany the merging of the seasons. Summer can be hateful with the shortage of water, fear of fires and screeching cicadas; but on breathless summer evenings when the moon is high, magpies carol a sleepy melody in the stillness. No other bird song is as lovely as this: it is indescribable and unforgettable.

...

Liebchen enjoyed moonlit hunts through grass at cat's eye level, creeping among slick nocturnal animals, where tree trunks were gigantic monsters whose spirits walked abroad at night, whilst the bark housed a thousand newts, beetles, spiders and little live things with scared eyes. She who was so domestic to us, so pretty, so interesting to watch or to caress, was a splendid hunter with a fierce light in yellow eyes, and her muscular body was lithe, supple and stealthy. On these terms, we must have seemed stupid and uninteresting to her: we who slept the night away and ruined the days cooking, ploughing or reading black and white pages of poetry or philosophy.

She did not always disdain the daylight for her barbarous killing. When the apples and almonds were in bloom in the orchard, and their branches were softly pink in the one case and purest white in the other, droves of rainbow lorikeets trooped down to us, showing off their clear reds and warm yellows, and busy-bodying about the lovely awakening trees. With their bright black eyes they are the sharpest of all the birds, except the minahs. Our beloved cat sat calmly waiting, sometimes springing a couple of feet into the air to kill her prey and inevitably returning with her catch. Sometimes she brought home rabbits, almost bigger than herself, growling furiously and stopping to shake them into dying submission when she found it difficult to carry her load.

Whenever she was 'in an interesting condition', Liebchen left off her night expeditions and hugged the fires, accepted enormous quantities of food and became the most domestic of cats. She came inside and chose places of vantage to sit — the wireless, on which always stood a vase of flowers fresh from the garden, or briar berries, or tall tufty grasses; she made a pretty picture and she loved our adoration. The sunlight fell on her there and the fresh breezes played on her soft fur, flattening it with a soft breath. Sometimes she sat on the edge of the table under the light, watching beetles she had become too lazy to catch, alert only at the prospect of milk. Or, turning her back on us, she sat on a sideboard, her tail softly switching as she faced books whose sober backs gave no indication of the riches within.

Leibchen could narrow her eyes to yellow-black slits and watch us with the unfathomable gaze of a Mona Lisa. She was soft and light when you lifted her up, but more determined and wild than you would ever dream. All her docility was soap in the eyes, because the scheme behind her posing was that a soft spot in somebody's wardrobe, an eiderdown, a cushion or the big blue easychair in the sitting room and kitchen were so much more comfortable to bring one's kittens into the world than the chill of the grain-barn or the chaff cutting shed. Heavy with her burden, she did not care to hunt, but accepted the amenities of civilization. Mother was usually right on her trail at these times and usually managed to persuade her that a worn-out sweater in a big box was a much better place. With all other places denied and her eyes mysteriously dark and urgent, she accepted this final refuge and achieved her kittens.

Not a single soul or thing was allowed near the sacred box that held her treasures, except we favoured four people. Mother declared that Leibchen was all mothers rolled into one; her kittens were the fattest, most well cared for babies in the world. Her family was almost always triplets, sometimes only two, the grossest error being four. Our cat became four times her normal size and fury incarnate if any unfortunate dog approached the vicinity. No dog ever did that on purpose; they always used judgement and discretion where Liebchen was concerned. Instead of being away all night hunting, she was focused on the care and nourishment of her precious babies.

...

This was not the usual Liebchen, who if inadvertently left inside at night silently tried all the windows as a means of exit. If this failed, as it could because of flywire protection, she walked from room to room, making the most appalling din, until one of us let her out. It was usually Mother, because my brother couldn't hear her in the sleepout, Father slept too soundly, and thunder could crack over my head and leave me oblivious. However, we all heard her at various times and the variation in her calls was amazing.

First came the entreating, 'Purr-ow!'

Next, a querying, 'Purr-ow!'

Becoming an imploring, 'Purr-ow!'

Finally, the demanding 'Purr-ow!' followed by noisy and miscalculated clumsy jumps about in the dark, which always brought about the desired effect. But, of course, the mother Liebchen, when all laps of refuge had gone to bed, artfully retired to the box of kittens and with classic beauty, moulded her little body about her babies. My brother used to visit her and cry like a kitten being ill-treated. This was one game in which she never joined and she always became most distressed if the heartless one continued his trickery.

When she weaned her family we had the most amusing time, because once she decided that fresh milk from the cows was sufficiently nourishing for them, she sat and growled and spat at these wondering kittens if they dared to approach. She did not melt at their mystified looks and hurt little faces: she had made up her mind and that was simply the end. She switched once more to her night huntress ways, returning in the morning fragrant with mint or briar.

People in the district often saw her in the bush on her daytime pursuits, and she was lucky not to become a pelt for some rabbiter who admired her fur or fall victim to traps, that fateful device that claimed many hunting cats. As the years passed she stayed longer and longer on these hunts, often a full week. My brother and I left home to live in cities and she seemed to miss our affection, which was so much more demonstrative than that of Mother and Father. Six hundred miles away, I used to hear from home and know all her movements.

Upon our return home, with the most unerring instinct, she would appear at the kitchen window and clamour to be let in. Even at the stretch of two years absence, there was no strangeness at the resumption of affection; Liebchen met us gladly, a chaste Diana, eager for the attention we loved to shower on her.

Chapter 6

Ethel

In her wildest dreams, she never imagined Theo's independence

While one might expect that Herbert and Ethel Fitzpatrick's move to Mannerim was a mutual decision, in the 1920s women didn't have economic independence. According to Marilyn Lake, 'many married women were subject to the gross or petty tyranny of husbands and the degradations of economic independence for them and their daughters.'[1] Moreover, Heather Radi's description of the expectations of women between 1920 and 1929, when Theo was finishing school and writing the story 'Liebchen', paints a very bleak picture:

> Women made up about a third of the workforce in the industrial states, as little as a sixth elsewhere. Perhaps they only found their place was in the home because prejudice about what constituted women's work denied them alternatives. Yet if that was so, they accepted the situation and the prejudice — and 55.6 per cent of male pay without obvious discontent. A few women stood for parliament just before the war, the first to be elected was Edith Cowan to the West Australian parliament in 1921, but by the end of the decade only three had followed suit. If anything, women's role in public affairs contracted during this period. Before the war a minority had been active politically, active in associations whose aims presaged political solutions, notably the temperance groups, active in trade unions and moving into the professions. Against an almost solid wall of disapproval in the twenties they seemed to give up.[2]

The Fitzpatricks' retirement to a Mannerim farm was not the idyllic existence one might have imagined from reading 'Liebchen'. Theo's workaholic father, incapable of relaxing and socialising, found himself with a wife who resisted the transition from 'baker's slave' to 'farmer's slave'; a wife who insisted on setting time aside for pleasure; a wife who read books, listened to music or wrote in her journal, while he milked cows, mended the fences and grubbed gum tree suckers from cleared paddocks from sunrise to sunset. For Ethel, who had little affinity with the land, the isolation of Mannerim after a life of interaction with people in a fashionable seaside resort was punishment, and her 1930s letters to Theo became a lifeline.

You seem to have grown up all at once

The Fitzpatricks lived in what is today an almost forgotten pocket of the Bellarine Peninsula. Progress was limited to bare essentials, with the Primary School No. 3096 name changed from Paywit South to Mannerim in 1911, and Mannerim's public hall built in 1925. The hall was near the station and the Methodist Church in Banks Road,[3] where Ethel Fitzpatrick played the organ, and the post office where she sometimes walked to post the letters from which the following extracts were taken, the first written to Theo two months before her twenty-first birthday.

Ethel encouraged Theo to qualify as an accountant, believing that qualifications were the key to success for a woman. With the same zeal, she discouraged any of Theo and Bill's relationships that she deemed unsuitable, believing that this was the recipe for a lifetime of misery.

Ethel's focus on her youngest daughter, out of reach, studying in Geelong, is constant, with early signs of her demands driving Theo away. Deeming it essential for Theo to have tertiary qualifications, Ethel deftly steered her clear of romantic entanglements. However, in her wildest dreams she could never have imagined Theo's future independent lifestyle.

30 June 1936

Dear Theo,

You will have had my motherly administration by this and I wanted to speak to you by phone today and waited over an hour in the bitter cold wind for that privilege. It seems hard to get to see you and I think I must harden my heart and get not to care, shall I?

There is a shaving brush reposing on a chrysanthemum bush in the yard, trying to pass itself off as a flower. Tell your friend that if he ever comes to Mannerim again, I have a hot water bag wherewith to put a little warmth into the sheets. I'm sorry I did not remember to do so.

July 1936

Dearest Theo,

I loved to see you lying across the foot of the bed talking in your quiet way of such intimate things.

I did notice one thing about your friend that needed a gulp to get over, which was that he says, 'By God.' In your promises at confirmation I see one is to keep the commandments, one of which is to 'Take not the name of the Lord Thy God in vain'.

8 October 1936

Dearest Theo,

While I think of it, prepare something for wearing under your evening frock at once in case you need to use it at short notice for you mustn't wear it again like that, now you are aware of its transparency. It was as if your legs were quite bare up to the scanties, and they (the scanties) could be seen quite plainly. You had such an enjoyable time, but I would have been happier if the frock had not been so transparent. Ever so many people have spoken to me about your dancing, and how you seem to have grown up all at once.

We were speaking about you coming home Saturday week, but there will be nothing on here that week. Would you like to leave it until the following week, on the 24th when there would be a dance at Mannerim?

Privileged women had choices by the 1920s

'Privileged women had choices by the 1920s,' said Anne Longmire. However, as she recorded in *The Catalysts: Change and Continuity 1910–2010*, a dilemma remained:

> The question of having to choose between marriage and a career remained unresolved, with most women wanting to marry despite the loss of many young men in World War One. However in the last decades of the 19th century and from the beginning of the 20th, there were alternative prospects of self emancipation available through tertiary education, application of newly formulated skills through the experience of specialised war work, and changing conventions in morality and social expectations.[4]

There was no indication whether or not Theo was planning to deviate from the predictable choice of marriage over career as she juggled living, working and studying in Geelong, with the obligatory, over-scrutinised weekends on the Fitzpatricks' farm:

Saturday 1937
Dearest Theo,

I wanted to see you so much this weekend, particularly as Geoff and Bessie are away at her people's (or so they say), and I asked Geoff to ring you and say so and that I would willingly pay your fare home. Did he do so today, as he promised?

I wanted to see you for I am fed up with Geoff's jokes about you not wanting to come. He is very petty. But these things have a nasty way of sticking as mud does. Often when he is angry he will say, 'Theo and Bill don't let you know what they think of you, they don't blurt it out as I do, but they tell *me*.' Beastly. Then I get miserable. I have tried to ignore it, but occasionally it gets me down.

I wrote to you one day last week, but Geoff took the stamp off the letter and used it for Bessie and said he gave you the letter.

When I knew the ball came off on Wednesday I fully expected a letter full of it or yourself to tell me all about it. I had a letter from Dulcie this morning in which she tells me you looked lovely, as I'm sure you did, and hope you had a happy time and that Scotty did not get too full and say foolish things as before.

Tuesday 1937
Dearest Theo,

Before I forget to give you the news, I must begin with it. First of all do you know of the feverish activities in search of so-called treasure, which many people believe to be a search for oil or coal, or something, which would really prove to be treasure. And wouldn't it be wonderful if that could come true? The Devlins at Marcus and Mr Bolton here at Mannerim have both given consent and the lease of a portion of their land for a search.

Now little daughter, about that subject so much on your mind: do not be in too great a hurry to settle matters. It would be better for you certainly. Could you talk matters over, but as things stand you would have to wait if monetary affairs were not suitable, for no-one can pay their way on love worse luck. However all these things are in your own hands. No one can help you in deciding such great matters. But as I have said, you have my blessing and my love. Were these things in my hand I suppose I should feel no-one was good enough for you. In any case I suppose a girl who has lived a good clean life should set a price upon herself: not commercially of course. But we'll talk some more later. I am so pleased at your confidence, darling.

29 June 1937
Dear Daughter,

I feel rather perturbed about you. There is such a thing as fascination and that is the only word I can think of to describe your feeling to Scotty as it appears to me. I would rather you did not show it so plainly and were more natural. Naturalness is wonderfully attractive, at least yours is, especially for those who know gold from dross.

I want you to think very seriously before you decide on your life's companion, if or when there is that necessity. I made a mistake that I would die to save you from making, and speaking is far from dying.

You are very young as regards experience of men, and men's ways, which can be fascinating. And I never can feel able to thoroughly trust a Churchman. You proved that to me once before when Scotty took you to (I believe) your first ball. He said many things then that he did not mean.

Anyway, I only want you to make very certain about love. Character, Disposition, Manners and Habits are so seriously to be considered and approved in making so momentous a decision.

On Sunday night, I could not help making quiet comparisons between the man I do not know and Mr Scott, i.e. Mr Turnbull, 'one of the strict sort who neither drinks nor dances', the former who smokes like a furnace, seeming to need so much sedative and who you thought drank too much at that first dance. All these things a mother 'ponders in her heart', as the Bible puts it.

Write a letter once a week

Drusilla Modjeska's biography *Poppy*, which is the story of her mother, helped her begin to unravel their complex mother-daughter relationship. To what extent, I wondered, were Theo's life choices made to escape from Ethel, through fear of becoming just like her mother? And like Drusilla Modjeska, who spent her life in Australia, far away from her mother in England, Theo collected and preserved her mother's writing. Here they differed, with Modjeska coming to understand her mother through writing the story of her life, while Theo left the ingredients of her mother's story to a trusted friend.

14 July 1937
Dearest Theo,

I intended to write tonight, but am too terribly tired. It was such a beautiful day that I was tempted to try the walk to the Post, to ring Dulcie, and to have a little yarn, and got properly knocked up. She was not at home, so the effort was futile, as in your case. You did not say why you were not there, whether your lunch hour was altered or when best to ring you if at all. I was very disappointed for I waited at the Post Office a long time to ring the second time. Cost ten pence, result nil and the long walk back.

At times I feel I would like to go away, away and never return. That feeling grows and gets so all-absorbing it might really happen. So sorry you're here for times of depression. But if you have a remedy, that's a big help.

Do you not think you could write a little bit — a letter once a week? This is a terrible separation to me. You have dances and entertainment, tho' you do not tell me of them. I always hear even that you did not go to Church on the Sunday evening you left here. Did you miss the bus that night? I thought you went back mainly for the service.

Thursday 1938

Dearest Daughter,

I really think that is what a *home* is for. To be able to talk just when one's heart and mind is full and one wants the safety valve to work. And too, that's what Mothers are for — tho' one of them is well aware that they cannot do much else but understand.

I think you know that for myself I do not go much to Church, but all the same if they really do teach Christ (not the Old Testament stuff, altho' that is good history of man's development) it is ideal. But people who try every day and all the time to live well ignoring all temptation to be led from right living and thinking, despite all there is to so gradually undermine our best spiritual instincts, shall I say? Are often more spiritually minded after all. For there is a very strong tendency, when one mixes with Church people, of becoming used to something less than we hoped from their association.

But do not lose hope, Darling. If one lives well, standing firm upon the feet in this unhappy world, putting aside all those things that help in the downfall of mankind, helping where we can, hoping always that goodness will triumph. Striving always for a firm grip upon the senses and spirit. Live well and you'll find an abundance of happiness deep down in your being that nothing can touch.

Bill wants me to try and persuade Dad to sell the farm and go and live in Hamilton. It is a good district and it would get us out of this little depression of nature. I get so tired of Geoff, who alternates between bullying and obliging. I want to feel mistress of my own home and I'll never be that while he is here.

I do love you so dearly little daughter, and prayerfully and lovingly watch over the unfolding of your life in all its phases. I love you to turn to me when you try to express your longings, hopes and fears, which come to all thoughtful people.

Chapter 7

Theo

Women climbing Cradle

Theodora Fitzpatrick climbed Cradle Mountain on her first trip to Tasmania in 1940. This was only four years after the explorer, conservationist and photographer Frederick Smithies, with members of the Northern Tasmanian Alpine Club, had set out to emulate the 1914 climb of Austrian brothers Franz and Julius Malcher while visiting their friend Gustav Weindorfer at his mountain chalet, called Waldheim.

Far from thinking about infiltrating a traditional bastion of men, Theo was anxious about her employment prospects as she waited for news of a temporary transfer to her company's Hobart office, which was still unconfirmed when she commenced the Cradle climb with her brother, Bill.

In a 1937 feature story, 'Skyline Climb on Cradle Mountain', Smithies described sporadic activity prior to his climb, with an amused comment on something out of the ordinary for the mid-thirties, the intrusion of a woman in what had been the sole domain of men:

> … most of the principal peaks have been climbed on different occasions, and a few, including at least one of the gentler sex, have traversed a greater part of the summit, no-one, so far as can be ascertained, had set out to emulate the feat of the Austrians until early 1936.[1]

Adversarial responses by self-appointed male 'experts' on women's nature and health were cited by Holmes and Tarr, as a prominent feature of the Belle Epoque:

> Despite the small scale of the feminist movement in France, a crisis in men's confidence in the solidity of the patriarchal order seems to have occurred, at least among the intellectuals. In essays, novels, lectures, plays and press articles men exhorted women to what they claimed (with some lack of logic) they inevitably and essentially were: kind, more concerned with the good of (male) others than with their own, gracefully passive, chaste, the guarantors of humane society not through any active political role but indirectly, by taming the brute that was one aspect of masculine strength. They waxed vehement on the dangers of any other course of female behaviour: women who wrote, voted, pursued their education too far would become sterile, hysterical or mad, while their men folk would become feminised and French civilisation would decay.[2]

While French intellectuals used pen and print in an effort to quell the uprising of what Smithies called 'the gentler sex', women in Australia, like Theodora, went about unwittingly, believing they had freedom and equality with men. What was more damaging to women's prolonged quest for equality was that twentieth-century women were kept ignorant of historic female landmark decisions, with the snail's pace progress of female equality missing from history books until 1970.

By the early forties, a few stalwart women regularly went bushwalking in the Tasmanian wilderness, expecting equal footing with men and leaving behind the Victorian patriarchal conventions that had limited the outdoor recreation of their mothers and grandmothers. This is part of what Holmes and Tarr describe as the 'Belle Epoque', the corresponding French 'first wave' of feminism that had swept the globe, articulating feminist issues that would run through the next century, translating into political action and protest.[3]

Chateau Waldheim at Cradle Mountain

10 January 1940

The Taroona passed up the Tamar with long ripples from the bow extending in lovely lines to break against the banks. We glided around curve after curve, with a succession of wooded hills, orchards and farms, and I was reminded of Chinese pleasure boats with windows of different shapes so the philosophers within might gaze at the passing pictures. My brother Bill and I had planned a sixty-mile walk through the little-publicised realm of unique mountainous beauty, Cradle Mountain and Lake St Clair Scenic Reserve.

When the Taroona reached Launceston, our friend Gwladys Morris, who we had had not seen for about five years, was waiting on the wharf. We three spent a hectic morning rushing about buying provisions for the trip and afternoon saw us on the train bound for Railton. And what quaint trains a three-foot-six gauge produces, we thought, as we whiled away the journey trying to decide whether the train whistled in thirds and fifths, or thirds and eights!

We passed through pleasant countryside where green undulating fields forever led the eye to a background of mountains, with masses of great clouds piled high to complete the picture. The mountains seen from Launceston are Mount Barrow 4644', Mount Arthur 3895' and Ben Lomond 5169', and after we passed the Western Junction Station, the Western Tiers came into view.

Near Railton, where we disembarked, rabbits calmly sampled the vegetation as the train rushed past. We looked about for the train to Sheffield and saw a tiny, self-conscious little train, standing on the opposite side of the platform and we packed ourselves into that. For all its lack of size, it efficiently climbed the steep grade into Sheffield where we were to stay the night. After tea in the hotel we went for a stroll, watching the play of evening purples deepening to richest blues on Mount Roland, which provides a beautiful, constantly changing backdrop to the little township. This farming district is renowned for its rich soil and the farmers appear to have a sense of the picturesque too, leaving windbreaks of clumps of trees in artistic positions. At this time of the year the paddocks were strewn with daisies and buttercups.

...

The next morning Os Connell arrived with the car, to take us to Chalet Waldheim at Cradle Mountain, forty miles from Sheffield. The morning was perfect, with the blue buttresses of Mount Roland standing out clearly beyond the paisley patterned fields. As we proceeded down the road, Mount Roland with the farmlands clustering at its feet, was left further and further behind, until we were in bush country. About fifteen miles from Waldheim we passed the Daisy Dell sawmills with workers' cottages strung along the road. We had occasional glimpses of Cradle Mountain, but it wasn't until we skirted the valley of the Dove River that we felt we'd arrived.

We spent four days at Waldheim; one of them climbing over Hanson's Peak to Twisted Lakes, which are tarns beneath Little Horn, one of the peaks of the Cradle. There were pencil pines at the edge of the lakes and we had lunch seated on the heather, which was in flower. On this day the weather was not particularly good to us and we fared better on the day we climbed the gentle grade up to Hounslow Heath, where there is a grandstand view of sorts. Across the golden button-grass valley we could see Cradle, Marion's Lookout, Hanson's Peak, and the glittering Dove and Crater Lakes.

On another afternoon we walked down the road to see Pencil Pine Falls, following the river downwards a short distance, to a pine forest hung with long festoons of pale-green and white moss. The boats on Crater and Dove were very enticing and we spent hours, either paddling about looking at the pandani trees, the richea and the fagus, which is Australia's only deciduous tree, or just simply sitting and gazing at the cliff walls of Crater Lake and the magnificent views of Cradle from Dove Lake.

On the day of our departure from Waldheim the sun smiled benignly, drinking up the tremulous mists of the valleys. The packhorse was to take our stores as far as Kia-Ora Creek, so we walked along unencumbered by rucksacks. The first stage of the journey is about twelve miles to Lake Windermere hut, but we decided to climb Cradle Mountain on the way.

From Marion's Lookout it was glorious, as mountain upon mountain swung into our ken, and we were like Cortez gazing at new worlds from the peaks of Darien. Once over the Marions, the peak of Cradle rose in grandeur from the level of the plateau, and Barn Bluff, some six miles distant, dominated the landscape with its squarish shape. It was such a wonderful place that if it rained for the rest of the walk it wouldn't have mattered: I had the memory of the green sweep of the plateau, the fragrant clear light air, the blue deeps of the sky, brown Cradle's ragged ramparts, and the serene blue of Barn Bluff, rising from the jungle growth of the depths of Fury Gorge.

The woman behind the man and the mountain

Waldheim's acknowledged founder, Gustav Weindorfer, who died in 1932, isn't mentioned in Theo's beautiful first impressions of the Cradle Mountain Reserve, but she couldn't have gone to Cradle Mountain and not have been aware of his legend. However, like the history of her fishermen and lifeboat ancestors, it wasn't entirely true. In the period that Theo was discovering the Tasmanian wilderness, the contribution of the female co-founder of Cradle Mountain had been lost.

Weindorfer had a wife, unmentioned on his grave, forgotten by all, until historian Sally Schnackenberg found her lonely grave with the curious words, 'Beloved wife of Gustav Weindorfer', and wrote the biography, *Kate Weindorfer: The Woman Behind the Man and the Mountain*. Schnackenberg documents Kate's role as a full partner in the Cradle Mountain venture, until illness forced the couple apart in 1914. She died in 1916.

> With regard to the role of women generally, Kate Weindorfer was unique. She was well educated and her interest in bushwalking

> and botany was developed long before she met Weindorfer … It was Weindorfer's vision of what could be achieved and Kate's total support of him combined with their mutual love of natural sciences that was the catalyst of the formation of the Cradle Mountain Reserve … Without Kate's involvement in Weindorfer's life it is doubtful that the Cradle Mountain-Lake St Clair National Park as we know it would be a reality today.[4]

As Theo set out to climb Cradle Mountain in 1940, she may not have known that in the first ten years of the Walheim Reserves, the most difficult years when the venture was literally carved from the wilderness,[5] Weindorfer was fully supported by his wife's finance, energy and inspiration. Waldheim was well established as a tourist destination and being promoted by the Northern Tasmanian Tourist Association in 1913, a year before the onset of Kate's terminal illness.

Theo climbing Cradle

What was deemed suitable attire for Theo, among the first women to tackle the Tasmanian wilderness, when there were no female role models to follow? She was young and she wouldn't want to appear dowdy, but she was adventurous too, and she had to be practical. Following a mishap on this Cradle climb, she quickly learned that proper footwear was essential to her wellbeing:

> Climbing Cradle was not the child's play it appeared to be, and we lost the cairns once we had climbed over the sky line, so that we spent two hours negotiating a slippery gulch of the most intimidating structure. Unfortunately I lost the heel of my boot in that unpleasant place, and was obliged to limp the rest of the many miles to Lake St Clair: so much for new chums attempting too much in a new land. Fearing to delay the party too much, we after all our hard work, were obliged to retrace our steps without gaining the pinnacle, and hungrily returned to the

Windermere track to devour the lunch which Gladys had prepared. With Cradle Mountain on the immediate left, and Barn Bluff on the right, the track winds through Pencil Pines, then through gums — snow gums, gnarled and twisted with the struggle for existence, and then through open heather moors, to the Cirque, from whence one gazes into the blue mountainous heart of the Reserve. There they stand, dreaming one more day of their thousand, thousand years of life: the everlasting hills. Clear in the afternoon light, opalescent in hue, from the outline of Western Bluff to the classical spires of Mount Ossa, and the faint, but thrilling tracery on the skyline of Frenchman's Cap. From the Cirque one sees the terraced valleys falling, mile on mile to the Forth Gorge, like some gigantic Zanadu pleasure-garden arranged for the delights of gods, not men.

Overlooking Lake Windermere

With a high vantage point, the climbers saw where they had come from and where they were going. As Theo wrote, it was all 'clear in the afternoon light'. But was it? At this point in her life, Theodora Ethel Fitzpatrick was standing on foundations carved by the feminist sisterhood. If knowledge of the past stops us making mistakes in the future, then Theo was starting her Tasmanian odyssey with a tactical blunder. While the significant lifestyle changes that came from broadening the scope of women's activities brought a new sense of identity that was denied her mother's generation, she was naïve if she thought that joining men in work and recreation gave her equality.

> Annelise Mauge identifies a crisis of male identity around the turn of the nineteenth and twentieth centuries, and interprets this as a reaction to a modernity that many men perceived as empowering for women, but as profoundly destructive of virility.[6]

Theo, whose life was in many ways remarkable, in failing to realise her full potential was no different to most of her generation and subsequent generations of young women who thought they were running laps on the main arena only to find at the end of their careers that they'd been on a treadmill all the time:

We left the Cirque to follow the track down through Waterfall Valley, and across the wonderful expanse of the golden moors, enclosed in the arms of which are many tarns, gleaming back blue to the blue sky, and over the rim of which the very tip of two mountains show: Pelion West and Mount Ossa. Barn Bluff had now changed its shape from dolerite cliff-faces to a long slope of rock and milligunya gardens, and a long ridge led up from the moor, giving the promise of an easy ascent — which we decline with thanks, at this stage of the proceedings. Passing from the sweeping lines of the moors and the feeling of suspension between heaven and earth, we paused for a moment on the ridge overlooking Lake Windermere, and once again there is the panorama of the mountains, suffused now with unbelievably lovely purples, and blues.

No arm clad in white samite waved thrice from the Lake when we reached it, but the appearance of the hut was very welcome, although the accommodation problem was rather acute, with insufficient bunks for everybody and two of the wayfarers were obliged to sleep in the loft. The walkers cook over huge open fireplaces in each hut, with everything provided. There are billies, frying-pans, washing-up utensils and an axe in every hut. Visitors are of course expected to extend the usual courtesy of leaving the huts with at least as much firewood as they use; and this is not difficult, for the huts have been judiciously placed as far as wood — and water — is concerned. It is of interest that some inexperienced walkers do not provide themselves with sleeping bags, but take blankets: the latter are not nearly as warm and have the disadvantage of being bulky and awkward to carry. The bunks in each hut are large, made of boards, and usually lined with dried button-grass.

At ten the next morning we were on our way again, but the day looked surly, with low clouds flying. The country, however, was very pleasing and after about a mile or so we were upon the open moor-country again, with Pelion West dominating the landscape to the middle right, and the imposing Mount Oakleigh rising from the depth of Forth Gorge on our left. On looking back Cradle Mountain smiled like Lorelei, and Barn Bluff looked sternly impressive, seeming far closer than Cradle. A dull day in the hills often produces the richest and most beautiful blues, and it was so this day. Forth Gorge is clad with forests of myrtle, and yet its whole length seemed dyed with blue; Mount Oakleigh is composed of brown dolerite rock of these regions, yet it bore a mantle of turquoise; Pelion East, readily identifiable by its sharp peak, rose in indigo beauty against the sky; Pelion West, now so close to us, swept up in strong lines from the mellow colour of the moor to pinnacles of blue.

On the narrow, winding track it was necessary to stop to appraise the beautiful scenery and the leeches of the area heartily approved of those who stood thus, lost in admiration. They came in undulating hordes, invading the boot-holes and trespassing on the flesh of the unwary. They are the police of these parts who say very effectively, 'Keep moving!' in no uncertain terms. Infested by these bandits, the path winds along the length of the base of Pelion West, and passing through a most lovely valley, entirely enclosed by mountains, rises again to the Pelion Plateau, on which the Pelion Huts are situated.

...

We seemed to spend a considerable amount of time just gazing around and it was eight o'clock before we arrived at the hut, a most commodious and sturdily built shelter, with benches in the porch on which diligent geologists had deposited trophies of rock marked with fern and shell indentations. We were hungry, but Dolly the packhorse had not arrived. At nine o'clock we were more hungry and weary. At ten o'clock more weary than hungry, we heard the cooee of the master of the packhorse. To our shame at eleven o'clock we were eating a large dinner, which was completed with plum pudding!

A bathe in the creek was advised by one of the visitors as being most refreshing: 'refreshing' was as gross an example of British understatement as could be ever imagined. It was *electrifying*, but most invigorating!

When the stunning effect of the first shock had passed, one became aware of the most consuming hunger. After breakfast we returned to the narrow path wending into the wilderness, following the track through the bush and up to the Pelion Divide. This little ridge is the natural and actual dividing point between the North and South portions of the Reserve.

Looking back in the Northerly direction from which we had come, we had our last glimpse of the now distant Cradle and Bluff; Oakleigh we would not see again from the track; but the gateway between Mount Pelion East and Mount Ossa is Pelion Divide, and we turned our faces to the South to discover new mountains — Cathedral, Falling, Massif, Ossa and Doris, each within a day's climbing of where we stood. Snow-poles marched across the heather beckoning South and the morning light played over the mountains highlighting the rocks and cliffs.

At the Kia-Ora Creek we parted from Dolly and her master, with a hearty handshake for the latter, and *auf wiedersehen* to both, as they were returning to Waldheim. We donned our packs and arrived at the Du Cane hut in good time for lunch, as the distance from Pelion Hut is only some six miles.

The Du Cane hut is situated close to the crystal-clear creek in a clearing of the myrtle forest. One carries the mug of coffee outside the hut and, seated on a little hillock of close-growing green grass, surveys cloud-shadows flying over the face of Cathedral Mountain, and breathes deeply of the sweet mountain air. After the sordid task of washing up we walked through the myrtle forest to the finger-post indicating Ferguson Falls, from which point the path plunges headlong downwards among the trees. But the scramble is well worth the trouble, for the Mersey has gouged out a path through the living rock, managing however to provide a natural rock-arch bridge for the walker, who then proceeds along the path to the falls.

Waterfalls are not one of my vices, but Ferguson Falls are really beautiful. Showers of white foam part to reveal a rock-shape not unlike a recumbent woman, and then the curtain of foam sweeps down into the narrow and deep path of water through the rocks. The Mersey River here is unchecked and lovely; how much less important and pristine it becomes as it nears the sea at Devonport when, absorbed in the service of commerce, it adopts a middle-aged spread.

. . .

The fourth day of the walk was to the Narcissus Hut, theoretically a distance of fourteen miles; to those unused to carrying rucksacks, hindered by a heel-less boot, and the consuming thirst of the chocolate-eating, inexperienced walker, it was not easy. If time were only as elastic as those fourteen miles! At first through myrtle forest, and then through gum-country winds the track. All day long we walked with the Du Canes to look at on our right, the names of the individual peaks sounding like a chant of vigorous joy; Falling Mountain, Massif Mountain, The Acropolis, Cyrean, Mount Gould, The Guardians, Mount Manfred, Mount Byron, Mount Olympus, Mount Ida and The Traveller's Range! Toward the latter part of this journey the park-like lands of the Narcissus River are reached and, crossing the stream, we spent some moments watching the trees bending in dreaming reflection over its limpid depths.

The combination of too much water drinking, and scenic-indigestion, found me a ruined woman the next day, so my brother Bill went off with Gladys to see Lake Marion. Somehow our food had nearly run out, but I searched among the cupboards and found some dried beans and bacon, and after a day's rest and meditation I managed to produce a stew for the rest of the party. They said it was delicious, but they must have been frightfully hungry. With great subtlety I kept them talking about their day, so they could not concentrate on the gastric monstrosity. They drew glowing pictures of the beauty of Lake Marion, above which the great cliffs of The Guardians rise.

. . .

The next day we walked through the fifteen miles of myrtle forest to Mr Fegusson's Tourist Camps at Lake St Clair. As we were walking along the path through the great trees, the sun shone in slanting shafts through the leaves, and fell dappled on the floor of the forest. We had frequent glimpses of the classical shape of Mount Ida, across the width of the lake. Each time we paused to look at the mountain we saw it differently framed: sometimes through tropical looking pandanni-trees, sometimes across a sandy beach curving between headlands of gigantic and mossy myrtles, sometimes solely through the fragile tracery of the myrtle tops. Among the knotted roots sometimes there were brilliant yellow or scarlet toadstools. When we reached the camp, Mr Fergusson made us very welcome and we enjoyed the luxury of a hot bath. We were jubilant at having a civilised dinner again after meals prepared in a billy, and to sleep the night in comfortable beds complete with snow-white linen.

On the day after reaching this lovely spot — for here Lake St Clair spreads out in blue beauty, watched over by Mount Ida and Mount Olympus, we walked up Mount Rufus, whose graceful outline sweeps upward to terminate in a wonderful peak. There were veritable gardens of richea in the valley before the final climb — richea with heavily laden spikes of flowers of all shades, from richest red to pure white. From the pinnacle we gazed upon the mountains at whose feet we had so recently walked.

At the camp I found a letter from the Company inviting me to come to Hobart for two or three months.

There was also a telegram, which said, 'Go to Queenstown, please.'

Another letter said, 'Don't go to Queenstown, come to Hobart.'

The last-dated of all was a telegram saying, 'Go to Queenstown.'

Since our luggage has become mislaid somewhere between Cradle Mountain and here, it seems I shall report for duty in Queenstown wearing a horrible red tartan skirt, walking boots with one heel missing and a rucksack on my back. It is rather sad saying goodbye to my brother who is returning to Melbourne immediately, but for the most it will only be for a couple of months.

Who were Theo's female role models?

While Theo mentions frequent glimpses of Mount Ida, the accomplishments of its namesake Ida McAulay, a Tasmanian suffragist, have become hidden in the mists of time. In 1894, when Theo's parents were in the first year of their marriage and Queenscliff bakery business, Ida McAulay was a bright light in a breakaway Hobart feminist group, the Itinerant Society. Not only did these women meet regularly to discuss literary subjects, writers, famous women and women's suffrage, McAulay organised a women's rifle club as well.[7]

Melissa Benn highlights the pressures that can narrow options for impressionable daughters today: 'If when they are growing up girls do not see a wide range of women doing a wide range of things — in life, in magazines, on television — but are instead subject to a dull diet of the same old thin, pretty girls, doing their thin, pretty thing, then this will limit their imaginations and daring.'[8]

Typical of progressive Australian womanhood of the 1940s, Theo doesn't appear to follow her mother as a role model. This could be Ethel's fault for drumming into her daughter that the worst possible scenario in life could be to end up like her mother. However, with no strong women held up for young girls to follow in the education system, the girl from the Victorian seaside resort, where Thwaites Walk is named after her male ancestors who manned the lifeboats, was metaphorically cast adrift in a sea of men.

Chapter 8

Theo

Independence and freedom, roaming on a bicycle

If you believe the claims of Sarah Bernhardt in 1896, the bicycle heralded a sexual revolution. 'The bicycle is on the way to transforming our way of life more deeply than you might think', she said. 'All these young women and girls who are devouring space are refusing domestic family life.'[1]

Bernhardt's dire predictions hadn't a hope in Hades of being realised, as only one precent of French cyclists in the 1890s were women. Neither were the killjoy warnings of the medical profession, who called the bicycle a 'sterility-machine' and hinted darkly about other dangers to women.[2]

Fashion revolution for women restricted by corsets

What did happen, like a breath of fresh air, was a fashion revolution for women who had long been hampered by restrictive corsets. This 1890s quote from a letter written home by a Scottish art student in Paris, was used by Holmes and Tarr to explain the transition from bicycle knickerbockers to bloomers:

> 'I bike a l'americaine, as the nicest French people do: a short skirt about 4 or 5 inches below the knee and long gaiters which go right to meet the knickerbockers in case of one's skirt blowing up. I always strap mine down.' Photographs show soberly clad women in similar skirts, or sometimes early versions of trousers

> or breeches. Bloomers, which became famous, were originally meant to be worn under skirts.[3]

In the Tasmanian Archives in Hobart, there are photos of two female bushwalkers climbing Tasmania's Mount Ossa in 1921, wearing ballooning gathered skirts. Comfortable casual clothing for women made few advances over the next thirty years. In the 1940s some women climbers still wrapped their legs in the 'putties' three women are shown wearing on a tea break at Cradle Mountain between 1925 and 1926.

People reacted in different ways to the sight of women enjoying outdoor recreation. It wasn't what Theo wore on her 1940s bicycle ride to Scottsdale that scandalised a Tasmanian gentleman she met on her journey:

I have spent the weekend on a bicycle. Went to Scottsdale on Saturday and had the most amusing adventures on the way. Toiling up a great hill an ancient lorry came up behind me, with rattles that could be heard from quite a distance, and stopped.

The driver lent out of his cabin and said, 'Going far?'

'Scottsdale.'

'I'll give you a lift for a few miles if you like.'

'Thanks very much.'

The bicycle was placed in the back of the truck, and I seated myself in the cabin of the chugging ruin. Sitting on the springless seat, next to the other passenger, an alert black-eyed terrier, I took stock of the driver. He had a ruddy weather-beaten face, keen blue eyes and judging by the dilapidated condition of the truck and the wheezy-engine, he made the contraption work by sheer willpower. As the countryside rolled by, I was pleased to have accepted the ride, as the grade was definitely stiff for many miles and though the aspect of the country was pleasing, it was hardly such to warrant such an uphill push.

'I thought you were a boy,' the driver offered, without blushing and notwithstanding that my locks were by no means boyishly cropped.

'Why are you going to Scottsdale?'

'Just to see the country — I left work early and I've been on the road since quarter past one. I'm going as far as Scottsdale tonight, then on to Lilydale and back to Launceston tomorrow.'

'Good heavens! Are you telling me that you're doing all this alone?'

'That's right — but I don't feel alone.'

He was silent for a while.

'You're a very silly girl,' he began again, 'you should go to the next police station and tell them where you're going and how long you'll be away — and ask them to give you a pistol while you're at it. You never know who you could meet in these lonely parts — look for yourself, there's not a farmhouse in sight; there hasn't been one for the last ten minutes and there won't be one for another four miles. Don't tell me it's common sense to go about alone.'

'This is Tasmania,' I replied easily. 'It is a hundred times safer over here than anywhere else.'

He wasn't swayed. 'If you take my advice you'll get yourself a revolver and keep the police informed of your movements.'

As the conversation had reached a stalemate, we switched the subject to guessing each other's ages, so that there were plenty of compliments on both sides. He was sixty, although he hardly looked fifty to me: a product of a peaceful isle where people wear their age gracefully. On the other hand, in his eyes, by hitchhiking alone, I was aging disgracefully. And normally reticent about my age I conceded when, starting at the lower end of the twenty-scale, he reached 'respectable' and 'independent' twenty-four. We discussed the war, the crops and his problems carrying wood from the bush into Launceston with shortages of petrol, tyres and spare parts.

His name was Mr H. Allen, which he pronounced Hallen. We chatted away about *Wuthering Heights* and Laurel and Hardy, which we had both seen several times. It was a most profitable meeting, as he is a cleaner or something at the Star Theatre, and now, whenever I want to see a show there, with a girlfriend or boyfriend, all I have to do is ring him up and he will get me a couple of passes, which will cost me exactly sixpence.

When we were seventeen miles from Launceston, Mr Hallen rattled away down a side-road to get some wood and I pedalled off through thinning gum forests giving way to cleared paddocks, through which I finally saw the stern scree and rock of Mount Barrow rising up before me. Barrow was eight miles away, and where the bush and foothills faded it dominated the landscape. The forest changed to myrtle and dog-wood and the road swung in a long arc to the right so that the mountain was seen from the opposite side to its typical Launceston aspect. The road first skirted the forest-side of a valley, passing a stream and farmlands before going up a valley with green roadside verges sprinkled with a milky way of white flowers and blue peaks rising across tawny paddocks framed by the occasional gum. I was very happy and sang to myself scales of all sorts.

It was so beautiful that I stopped to look, at that moment in complete agreement with Robert Louis Stevenson, when he said that a man who lived in the plains country was forced to search for beauty in such things as 'cobwebs' and 'dew bediamonded', while he who lived near a mountain had merely to gaze at ever changing loveliness.

...

During my meditative pause I became aware of the patter of many little feet on the road and in a few minutes a flock of sheep arrived. What a happy inclusion in the picture, I gloated, leaning comfortably on the cycle, the better to see the white mass moving through the pastoral scene. However, their shepherd also appeared. An old man with a shock of perfectly white hair and cheeks as rosy as a Jonathan apple, he sat in a cart drawn by a white horse, which drowsy with the slow task of following the sheep, plodded quietly along with down-bent head. In the cart, beside the shepherd's feet, were two lambs.

'Good afternoon,' he called.

I smiled, returning the greeting, and once again that afternoon I had to practically give my full pedigree.

He began by asking, 'Well, where are you going to, Girl?'

He called me Girl the whole time, which rejuvenated me. Apparently he was tired of the company of sheep, for in the ensuing conversation he discovered, not only my age, but where I lived, worked and what my interests were. All these personal questions were asked with such simple directness that my answers were returned with equally simple frankness. His sheep took advantage of our preoccupation, scattering along the roadside to graze and had we not seen a car approaching in the distance we would have still been standing there, I'm sure. As it was, we parted positively old friends!

...

The road became steep up the ridge in a section known as The Sidling and the swoop down the other side precluded any attempt to enjoy the view. I owe my life solely to the fact that there was no other traffic on the road. The speed was exhilarating and that was four miles, or so, of down-hill-and-be-damned! When the road flattened out, I found myself in the rich, extensive farmlands of Scottsdale, with Mount Barrow now well in the distance.

At Scottsdale, I found a hotel where a crowd was noisily indulging in the Saturday afternoon pastime of spotting. Escaping from the hubbub, I stayed in my allocated room until dinner when I entered a lively conversation covering literature, socialism, communism, music, art, Tasmania, walking and skiing with the three people with whom I was placed, including a Howard Dalton, the parliamentarian's son, or should it be D'Alton? The group were pleasant to breakfast with as well, and I was sorry to leave.

Sunday morning saw me early on the road, and if you ever hear of anyone cycling from Scottsdale to Lilydale to Launceston, you may take it from me that they are crazy. It was frightfully hilly, and one walks up hills and then has to walk down hills, because the unsealed roads are too rough to ride on. I didn't enjoy the morning because I didn't quite know where I was for the whole trip until I hit the bitumen. There were no signposts to indicate the road to Lilydale. The war-time edict of removing signs had reached these outlying parts and it was necessary to check up on the road, asking as many people possible while there were still farmhouses about.

While the road was in a very poor condition, the impressive forest with tall, well-spaced gums, interspersed with bracken and scrub, made the hard going worthwhile. That was until I saw, coming towards me, a tall, spare figure, carrying an axe over his shoulder, and too late, remembered the previous day's advice to pack a revolver.

He stopped and watched my approach. He waited with his lean, tan face impassive; his dog not greeting me, but standing motionless at his side until I finally reached them. I summoned the brightest smile — secretly thinking it would be my last smile on earth, and asked if I was on the right road for Lilydale. Thereupon he grinned, easy and friendly, and recommended what turned out to be a worthwhile shortcut up the railway line. This was an easy grade up a long hill and as it steepened, I looked down on trees and wooded gullies, until I emerged at the top to see a sweeping expanse of sheep-grazing land. Upland pastures are a particular thrill of mine; the solitude, the expanse of sky and pasture, the elemental simplicity invariably charms me to contentment.

Coming from the brown fastness, on the Bellarine Peninsula in Victoria, to the rich, green farmland around Lilydale was a pleasing contrast. And after the long gradient leading up to Lilydale, the downside was another glorious swoop, when my faithful cycle took wings and bore me downwards with reckless joy. There was no mending kit on the bike and luckily, as the tyres were rather thin, a kit was never required.

Twelve miles from Launceston I discovered that I could ride with my hands in my pockets and I pedalled along happily, oblivious that my face was streaked with grimy perspiration. The 'no-hands' riding method was almost my undoing when *swoosh*, a young man rode alongside and I swerved and wobbled, perilously close to a collision on one of the last hills. He had no teeth on the top row, he sported a little black moustache and his hat had a curious serrated appearance. We came down the hill at a rattling pace. He of course adopted me, dirty face and all and had to peddle like mad to keep up with me, because my bike is heavy and when it gets the old eleven stone on it, we know what to do on a hill.

Well, this gentleman made the most lovable remarks, such as he wished that there were a lot of uphills because then the journey would go on for much longer than if it were all downhill. And that he had never seen a girl ride down any hills as fast as I went, and did I ever go to the theatre, because if so wouldn't he be lucky to be able to take me to see a show. And was I married? If not there was hope for him yet! What a ride! There's absolutely nothing like being on a bicycle for making acquaintances rapidly!

My love to anyone you meet who knows me

Following the weekend bicycle ride to Mount Barrow, while working at CPL Distribution in Launceston, Theo typed a letter to Nancy in Hobart on apricot-coloured paper, including some personal details omitted from her unpublished book. She finished in longhand, writing in black ink:

30 November 1942

I am reading G. K. Chesterton's, 'Alarms and Discussions'. Although the style is pithy and pleasing, the subject matter doesn't please me. I can think of far better essayists. I shall read more of GKC in order to become more familiar with this famous critic, who is impressive as a writer of the grotesque style. Next weekend I'm going yachting down the river, or, rather, paddling a boat back. My love to anyone you meet who knows me, provided you tell me who they are!

Chapter 9

Ethel

Rejecting the submissive role patriarchy reserved for her

Finally in step with feminism in the 1940s, Ethel Fitzpatrick had grown into the classic character described by the author of *Sexual Textual Politics*, 'Behind the angel lurks a monster.' We catch sight of this new person in her writing, with glimpses of someone akin to that admirable creature described by Toril Moi: 'The monster woman is the woman who refuses to be selfless, acts on her own initiative, who has a story to tell — in short, a woman who rejects the submissive role patriarchy has reserved for her.'[1]

Ethel didn't suffer fools gladly. Just as she couldn't hold back her honest opinion of the drunken Scotty in her 1930s letters to Theo, she doesn't mince words in her 1940s diary, where a duplicitous, stronger, less accommodating Ethel emerges. She is the ultimate warrior woman, celebrating her seventieth birthday on 31 July 1945, coinciding with the end of World War II, and sandwiched between V-E Day on 8 May 1945 and V-J Day on 15 August 1945.

Melissa Benn captures the phenomena of Ethel and all womankind when she nails the misunderstood demonic rage of a mother, a mother-in-law, a nanna, a grandmother or an auntie, that is time and again used against them. A rage that confuses all and sundry who are prone to believe that their older female relations are no longer lovable, nor deserving of respect:

> Anger often comes into its own when a woman is older, moving towards or passing the final 'breakpoint' of middle age: menopause.

> It's as if she suddenly meets her pre-pubertal self again, gazing clear-eyed out at the world as it really is, less preoccupied now with how the world sees her. The years of intricate connections and compromise, around sex, love and family, are not exactly behind her, but they no longer feel quite so pressing.[2]

Weeping at World War II on the wireless

Instead of crying 'ditch the witch' or walking on the other side of the road to pass their homes, Benn's words shine a compassionate light on the predicament of women who, having raised families, have seemingly lost their footing on the shores of an uncharted coastline. When their whole being is geared to nurturing, how does someone like Ethel stem the tears, stop the pain and fill the emptiness?

24 January 1941

This afternoon I sat in my chair beside the wireless set and listened to the description of the march through the City of the different regiments and divisions of the Royal Australian fighting men. Herb is among them and I was quietly weeping, as I imagined I could see him proudly stepping along with his unit.

The news of the Australians' dash and courage in the capture of Bardia and Tobruk have filled the men (and women too, but especially the men) with pride and eagerness to participate. I know that Herb longs to be in it, and I know too that we depend on them for our existence, but it is a saddening thought that there should be a need for war. How could I help crying when my mind went back to the morning he was born, on his father's birthday, when his father told me there were not many women so clever as to give their husband their first son for a birthday present.

At last the long drought has broken and the rain is filling Mannerim's empty waterholes. It was pitiful to see animals standing waiting patiently for a drink, with water carted to them from the water supply standpipe. Animals need so much water.

This weather, though so welcome, brings mournful thoughts. Is life worthwhile? One by one the children go from home and we are left alone, just where we started from. Where are they now — the seven of them? Dulcie married and widowed, with two sons; Herb married, childless and going overseas to fight; Mavis dead; Harold dead; Geoffrey married; Bill, single and teaching; Theo doing office work in Tasmania — how anxious I was that Theo should be trained to be independent. The idea of her being free to go far from home never presented itself. I should so much have liked her about me in my old age. Yet I do realise that the freedom to see other places and form her own friendships will broaden her outlook. Today I miss them all, try as I will to convince myself that this is the way of life.

26 January 1941

I have missed Theo terribly this Christmas time. She has always been such a darling to me. Her love and understanding is very precious. Dulcie, too, is such a loving girl, generous and impulsive, but there is something that distracts and irritatingly annoys when in close contact with her, that is past understanding. When she is away, somehow I can see her in true perspective. All her good qualities stand out and she is so lovable.

With Theo it is so different. She has fun with me, and laughs at my English ways, as she calls them. Cheats when we play cards, openly defying me to detect her. But we love and understand one another much, I fear, to make jealousy among other members of the family. That is unavoidable.

Poor women don't count in the scheme of things

Melissa Benn captures Ethel's feelings exactly in *What Should We Tell Our Daughters?* We can feel the simmering, volcanic rage of Ethel close to the surface, threatening to explode. All the more potent, Benn says, 'when expressed by those who have loyally played their part or played the game, only to find themselves thrown off course by what they know to be rank injustice.'[3]

6 February 1941

I have been quietly considering the tremendous differences that Money (with a capital or indeed all capital letters) makes in the world. Where I am it is looked up to and worshipped as the supreme thing in life. It is too in many ways, but to have it so constantly in mind, to have all ones thoughts on the importance of getting it, is to the extent of forcing out all love for good things we might and could enjoy. Those things which are free to all, however poor, is wrong is warping.

Yet how well I know what a big difference it makes to have money to make gifts both of money and useful presents. It is galling. And to be compared to those who have more and to be considered mean is equally galling. To bear these things in silence too is rather distracting, but to be *able* to do so, in whatever spirit needs real grit. (I often really do grit my teeth and try to carry on.)

I think this morning of Herb sailing, as Rene said last night, 'further and further away'. I've no doubt if all goes well he will be enjoying the trip, for he loves the sea. It is strange to hear consolations from all and sundry given to the wife and to hear so and so's son has gone and how much she must feel it and none at all offered to me (though I think I should resent it). You see, I'm poor, therefore, as must follow, I do not count in the scheme of things: strange, but so terribly true.

It is quiet here this evening, crickets singing, water spraying on the lawn, Scotty lying at my feet, deeply interested in the slightest movement in any direction. How nervous dogs are, he trembles when he hears a neighbour's gate close, because she often takes him for a run. A dog barking in the distance, a man's footfall or whistle has the same effect.

Herb sailed on the fifth. We believe the ship went out The Heads at 6am or thereabouts. The date of sailing was very vague, the danger of enemy action making it so. Yet to hear the people chattering about the probable date is terrible, in the face of all warnings to keep a still tongue, the mothers and wives of these men seem unable to hold their tongues, frequently discuss it, indeed, seem to be always talking.

21 February 1941

It is good to have the house to ourselves again. No matter how decent people are, it disturbs the peace and privacy of a private home. When people cater for boarders they have their own private rooms, but in a small place like this it isn't at all suitable and after two years of it I appreciate the home atmosphere again.

In a place like this there are many lonely hours, yet when I am in a city where all the houses are so close, privacy is impossible. Go out the back door and there are people on either side to see and to hear. The silly rubbish and gossip they talk about is nothing short of horrible.

14 March 1941

We are still in doubt about Herb's destination, although there is every possibility it is Egypt, with his ship stopping at Bombay. On Sunday it is the Church Harvest Festival and once again I will have the problem of dodging the notes that do not sound in that old organ. I am feeling more and more that I must give it up. It is a poor state of affairs that these people let their Church go to ruin: the floor is rotten and the outhouse is tumbling down and it is never cleaned or dusted. They are neither willing to have it closed, nor to maintain it in a respectable state and they call it 'the house of God'?

Knitting goes on apace and I am concentrating on balaclavas, which you see being worn in all the pictures of airmen and the men in the desert, which is unbearably hot in the daytime and the reverse at night. At the Harvest Festival I played for a lady singing 'Thanks be to God'. She had a beautiful contralto voice and even the preacher seemed better than usual. Perhaps it was the effect of the solo.

The memory of Mabel Mavis Fitzpatrick

You can see in Ethel's 1940s diaries that she didn't have the same easy rapport with her eldest daughter, Dulcie, that she had with her youngest daughter, Theo. Dulcie's husband died on 14 November 1936, when her sons, Winston and John, were seventeen and fifteen. She was seriously depressed for many years afterwards.

17 March 1941

I lay awake for hours last night, which is a usual occurrence with me of late, and thought about Mavis. How wonderful it would be if there were a realm of the Spirit, where we can meet and words are not necessary. Clear vision: perfect understanding. If she knows anything, she knows how I have repented any harsh words, spoken in anger, when I was being goaded into work, in pregnancy, in nursing young babies and trying to bear the burden of catering for food and clothes for a family on a pittance and being censored and bullied for not being able to do so.

Some men have a lot to answer for. I had to miss the sweetness of close companionship with my eldest children, to their detriment and mine.

Do you think I'm an angel?

Close on the heels of Dulcie losing husband Colin came the Second World War, with Dulcie's closest sibling and last connection with her Queenscliff childhood, her brother Herbert, posted overseas on active service in the army. Ethel doesn't mention in her 1940s diaries that Dulcie's son, her grandson John, was in the air force from 1941 to 1946. He began as a wireless operator and concluded his service as a Sergeant Linguist. He served in Darwin translating Japanese documents, and was sent to Tokyo at the end of the war as a translator.

24 March 1941

Strangely enough just now, in thinking of in-laws, Shaw's little bit in *How He Lied to Her Husband* came to my mind.

He, 'Have you sisters-in-law?'

She, 'Of course I have. Do you think I'm an angel?'

Oh, what would we do without books? I'm positive that I would be a raving lunatic, or perhaps, alternatively, a good farmer's wife, feeding pigs and poultry and milking cows, until being too weary to get out of bed one morning, I would just stay there and fade out.

5 June 1941

I know many mothers are suffering the frightful nervous strain of waiting for news and realise that it is far worse for the men themselves, in such peril as they are. This is no time for escape into reading. One cannot concentrate, and so day follows day in absorbing news from papers and wireless.

Our most damnable nature follows each child as part of our lives, we rejoice, are sad, happy or suffering, with each member of the family. I often think that children little know how a mother lives and moves in them, no matter where they are or what their work and way of life is. We can't help it.

'And Mary pondered all these things in her heart.' That little quotation often comes into my mind, and how well it is understood by millions of mothers the world over. Yet when I look at Bert absorbed in animals and the futile effort to make a little money, going from before daylight to after dusk, I would rather be a mother any day.

8 November 1941

Whether I had dreamt about Bill I do not know, but something awakened me at two o'clock in the morning, wondering if I had forgotten his thirty-first birthday. I felt impelled to get up and check the date, and found it was the sixth of November. Morning saw me waiting at the crossroads at nine o'clock for someone — anyone, going to the post office, so that I could send him a congratulatory telegram. Some strange things happen, like the time when he was born. He was not expected for another week, but Geoffrey threw a firecracker near me on Guy Fawkes Day, which precipitated Bill into the world seven days before he was due. I often wonder if the shock altered his life and temperament.

The year has passed quickly here. I had a letter from Herb and he says that there is only one place in the world he is longing to see. It is easy to guess where. He is full of fun, in spite of that longing, and makes light of the dangers and horrors connected with war. We live from hour to hour listening to news broadcasts, waiting for letters, writing letters and trying to follow all the moves of our fighting forces. The sinking of the *Sydney* so near to Australia filled us with gloom. The whole ships' company was lost with not a single one left to tell the tale of her last encounter with the enemy. Strange that no boats were found — nothing but a float and a lifebuoy.

The pleasure of Theo's homecoming in December is rather absorbing. I shall love to see her again after such a long separation. Two years means a lot in my life now.

Ethel's powerful persona threatened to take over

Ethel Fitzpatrick's powerful persona always threatened to take centrestage of what started as Theo's story. Through her writing we discover the strong Thwaites women and the foundation that launched her independent, free-spirited youngest daughter. Ethel's reminiscences show who Theodora was and how, when, where and why she came into being. But I still hadn't heard the last of Ethel. While packing the research material away to return it, I noticed a twenty-four page short story she'd written over seventy years ago, in flowing blue ink on cream writing paper, held together with a large, rusted safety pin.

One wonders whether Ethel was being extremely careful, burying her lingering grief for Mavis in this late-thirties short story entitled 'Recuperating in the Country', where it was unlikely to be discovered by Dulcie. What great losses they both had.

Or then again did Ethel, who wrote in a male voice, want to be discovered? Was she acknowledging the suffering of husband Herbert and the constant sons, Geoffrey and Bill? Was she saying, 'I know I've spent a huge hunk of my life missing Mavis, worrying about Dulcie and doting on Theo, but you were grieving too, and I'm sorry'?

Look at those clouds, floating in that sky as blue as a baby's eyes. As blue as my baby's eyes — I love that kind of blue. I always think of it as heavenly blue. Ah, but she's gone so long ago. If only I could believe she had gone to a beautiful place, where she would grow up and become one of God's angels, I would walk this earth with a sort of triumph. But I can't believe that the sweet little body of my Dora, that I saw the beginning of decay in, is going to become an angel. Somehow I can't believe it.

Perhaps it's my own fault, but there you are. I remember how my wife used to say, 'You must have been born with a maggot in your brain.' Might be so, too. Anyway, she believed alright and seemed quite happy about it after a year or so. Funny how we suffer or are happy according to our feelings.

I'll never forget her, but it's no good to be always moping and miserable. You can't work properly and it affects your health. And tho' I can love beautiful sights like those red roads running to the bay, along the shore and up the hill, that bit of forest over there, the homesteads sitting pretty looking over the bay, there's a feeling of loss behind it all that will always be there to the end of my days.

Oh, yes! A blue-eyed lass, fair hair, like gold it was. If God knows everything and gives us happiness in these things whatever did he want to take her away for? Oh no, I don't think he knows anything about what we feel and what we don't feel if you ask me. But there you'll be tired of hearing me talk so much, but I feel sort of bewildered about it all.

'Recuperating in the Country' is an empowered short story, laced with comic irony, as Ethel Fitzpatrick attributes long-suppressed thoughts and feelings to a male voice. She wanted to be heard, but nobody was listening. Does this demonstrate frustration at the limitations placed on an opinionated female in a patriarchal society, or is it something more complex?

> Women, even though they could not be mates, were to be treated decently but quickly put down if they showed any intellectual aspirations. In a leading article headed 'The Great Woman Question', the Bulletin offered the view of most nineteenth-century Australian men: 'the equality argument is an absurd one. Women are far from that progressive rationalism when they can take their stand on the same platform as men. Women, as totality, are far inferior to men, as a totality.[4]

In a masterful stroke, Ethel doesn't give the place a name: merely the last letter of the alphabet, which suggests isolation, a backwater, the extremities or the end of the earth. It is however in sight of the sea and near a lively place called Queensbridge, and these places are easily identifiable as Mannerim and Queenscliff. The visit of the talkative Queensbridge woman, Mrs Westgarth, and the arrival of the gentleman on the road asking directions, provides a discordant note. Who is really 'rusting' in the country? Is it Ethel, who was born in 1875 and watched the Queenscliff building boom? Is it Ethel, raised in a family of six girls and three boys at Fishermen's Flat? Is it Ethel, who served throngs of tourists and locals in the Fitzpatricks' Queenscliff bakery? Is it Ethel, the mother of seven children in an empty nest? Is it Ethel, the wife with the wrong husband?

Raised in the sophisticated seaside resort of Queenscliff, Ethel Fitzpatrick has experienced a culture shock moving to the farming community of Mannerim. She is not alone in her predicament as we see Henry Handel Richardson has experienced a similar reaction, not to local farmers, but to reading Thomas Hardy:

> Three other books I remember for a different reason. These were loaned me as a special favour from the 'Mechanics' Institute', and two I chose simply for their lovely titles: Under the Greenwood Tree and Far from the Madding Crowd. But Hardy's gnarled prose, together with the outlandish speech of his country-folk, defeated me.[5]

The characters in 'Recuperating in the Country' could have stepped straight out of a Thomas Hardy novel. At the very time the farmers of Dorset and Somerset were in mass exodus to Australia, a significant number settling in the Bellarine Peninsula, Hardy was consciously preserving the vanishing details of their lives. With agriculture mechanised, new employment patterns had emerged and their old communities were crumbling.

We are told in Ethel Fitzpatrick's short story that the local men gossiped and the women didn't. Peter, from the Country Roads Board camp, suggested that the women were afraid to speak. In such a significant body of writing, and not withstanding that the Fitzpatricks lost everything in a house fire at Mannerim, there is scant reference to the life and death of Harold and Mavis. The feeling of something missing persisted long after I had peeled apart some glued pages in Ethel's 1940s diaries and found the name Mavis on two more-or-less illegible pages.

Following the loss of two teenage children, I expected some elegiac writing from Ethel and her silence was out of character. When I finally found what I believe is an elegy to Mavis in the middle of 'Recuperating in the Country', the only imaginable explanation for her reticence and secrecy remained academic.

With the erosion of rural cultures, such as still existed in Mannerim in the late 1930s, the cultural space for mourning and grief, particularly in the seaside resort of Queenscliff where the Fitzpatricks lived at the time, had shrunk. Modern elegy's psycho-poetic history is outlined in Ramazani's *Poetry of Mourning*. An 1899 journal article by Joseph Jacobs described the period from 1880 to 1920, when the period of mourning was gradually shortened in Britain and America to a couple of days after the funeral, as 'The Dying of Death'. He blamed the lack of space for mourning's psychological necessities on the fast pace of modern life, a decline in religion and an increase in lifespan. Historian

Philippe Aries claimed that Western society had banished death, and a social anthropologist of the fifties and sixties, Geoffrey Gorer, argued that this denial had become a Protestant tradition, with the exception, it was observed by Aries, of the death of a statesman.[6]

Was Ethel gagged by this convention? What had I missed that made her loss so unspeakable that she needed to hide her grief in this surreptitious fashion?

Chapter 10

Theo and Ethel

WWII and the composing genius of Bach and Sutherland

Theodora's feet usually remained firmly on the ground. In fact, she was so well-grounded it was a challenge to get her to change course. But whenever she did there was no great drama, and she took everything in her stride. In November 1942, Theo's return flight from Melbourne to Launceston was typically followed by a succession of outdoor weekends, beginning with skiing at Ben Lomond. While exact dates are almost non-existent in Theo's Tasmanian story, wherever possible her writing is cross-referenced with her dated letters to family and friends.

November 1942

Returned from Melbourne yesterday evening by plane with visibility very clear until we came in sight of the Tasmanian coast, where we seemed to lose a good deal of height and flew just above heavy banks of clouds. A rainbow chased us on the left-hand wing, and save for the scrolled curves of poised cloud and glimpses of blue sea through sudden gaps, the cloud-banks were very like skiing fields. And then the glittering silver wing swung over the little hedged fields and the paisley pattern of the farming-district unfolded with the George Town Road running in a determined strip of blue right into, and through, Launceston. The wing dipped — would it clear the train, shunting so that it seemed like a clumsy kitten backing out of our majestic way? A new note to the engine, a slight bump and we were down. No longer Gulliver gazing on toy houses: but five-feet-six, and attached with remarkable tenacity to terra firma.

Singapore fallen and finished *The Life of Bach*

Around the time Ethel Fitzpatrick was reading *The Life of Bach*, two female musician friends of the composer Margaret Sutherland gave her some well-deserved encouragement, joining her in Melbourne to present a Brahms Sonata, *La Sicilienne* by Bach and *The Poised Fountain* by Bax.[1] While there is no connection between Fitzpatrick and Sutherland, we have already noted their similar marriage experiences and the need to recuperate traditions that link women together. It is interesting that Ethel's comments about Bach are also true of the composer Sutherland.

10 February 1942

I'm very interested in *As We Were*, by Benson. It is a great bit of character sketching, and his familiarity with famous people in different walks of life, from royalty, the Church, literature and art, make very entertaining and instructive reading. His word picture of Queen Victoria is much as I had it from my mother and is therefore familiar to me. It is as I had always had her image in my mind. The description of the gorgeous ceremony of her Jubilee and her own quiet, dignified entry, dressed in plain black and white was most impressive and brings back to me the day in which I read the report in the papers to my own mother, so long dust.

Rene has invited me to go to her in the event of evacuation from here. It's hard to know what to do. Neither of the other sons made any suggestions, which looks as though they mean me to take whatever comes my way.

16 February 1942

Still more reverses. Singapore, which we were led to believe would never fall, has gone. Hong Kong and Singapore, two naval strongholds, are taken. What next are we to expect? It is true that we are fighting a cruel and ruthless enemy, and a mighty combination of enemies, France, Germany, Italy, Japan, are all being used for making war material and for manpower. No wonder the old people are ill. To see the young and strong manhood of a nation like ourselves slaughtered is frightful, and those of us with sons and relatives suffer with them.

Have just finished reading *The Life of Bach*. There seems no doubt of the fact of a genius not being recognised during their lifetime. Bach was dead a century before his real worth was recognised. The misunderstanding and lack of appreciation he encountered was enough to kill his composing power. Yet it was so great and absorbing that no amount of discouragement stopped the flow of music, the source of which was in his very soul.

I am so grateful and thankful for books. Those we have here belong mostly to Bill, some are Theo's and many given to me by the children. I would much prefer to collect books than china. I like nice china, but with books one can dip into them at all times and find something to suit every mood. In these critical days, when the war news comes first and is always in ones thoughts, it is wonderful to snatch an hour or so to read much of what was written in the quiet days of peace.

24 February 1942

Shaw is refreshing. In *Man and Superman*, his characterisation is wonderful. The two guardians of Ann, so different, so absolutely under her thumb, the shrewd sayings of Tanner. For instance, when Tavy said that to marry Ann would be happiness for life, Tanner said that happiness forever would be hell.

I began this play last night and I'm going to enjoy it, war or no war. All the same, one can't but feel apprehensive. We live so near the coast that, should the Japs blitz us, we couldn't escape bombing.

Darwin and Broome have been bombed

On the one hand there was Theo, inexplicably drawn to her Tasmanian eyrie, and on the other her mother Ethel, at times withdrawn, disconsolate and lonely in pastoral Mannerim, on the Swan Bay side of seaside Queenscliff, in the Victorian Bellarine Peninsula, writing in her diary.

10 March 1942

Still the Japanese advance. Darwin and Broome have been bombed and if we do not get an immense lot of war material and airmen, we will be in for a lot of trouble in Australia. When one sees the mistakes that have been made and the lessons unlearned in this war, one feels a sense of almost fatality in looking ahead. If only we could feel confidence in our leaders, it would hearten us even against reverses. But when one blunder succeeds the same sort of blunder, one's confidence wavers.

The escape and return of Col Bennet leaves one perturbed. Should he have left his men? Couldn't someone else have been sent with the important news he had to tell? Did he merely save his own skin? One can only conjecture, but it leaves one with an uneasy feeling.

We look anxiously for a letter from Herb. According to the papers there is no enemy action in Syria, or at least, no mention of it. So we feel that delay is due to mail service, since no airmail is forwarded at present.

6 April 1942

Theo's news of her promotion to assistant manager of the Launceston branch of Chartres Ltd came a few days ago. She is thrilled with the news. She has worked hard and deserves success if anyone does. If only I could be near her, if only near enough for her to run in occasionally, life would hold more interest for me. It is strange, after years of intense thought for a family to find oneself stranded, so to speak. Wholehearted devotion to a family is not all it's cracked up to be. The family grow up, and grow away, as well as *go* away from you. Are all families like that?

India is proving herself a thorn in the side of Britain in this war. Britain's plans for a free India, considered so generous by other nations, are apparently not satisfactory to the Indians. It seems that with nations as with individuals, when the chance presents itself, to demand as much as possible. War is revealing of both nations and individuals.

Heroes and heroines at Mannerim

There is no hint of speculation from Ethel Fitzpatrick's self-absorbed daughter, Theo, about the unrealised potential of her mother. The onlooker watches the mother-daughter relationship of Ethel and Theodora becoming more and more one-sided:

> In Les Mots pour le dire, for example, the narrator interprets her mother's life as one of creative frustration as a result of the inactivity that her epoch and her social class impose upon women: 'She was aware that she should have lived for a certain aesthetic construction that would have been distinctively hers and which will never be defined. Would she have been a potter? An architect? A sculptress? A surgeon? Or a gardener?'[2]

With the Fitzpatricks' fiftieth wedding anniversary on the horizon, Ethel starts soul-searching in earnest.

8 April 1942

Still enjoying old Carlyle. He gives one some great thoughts. In a lecture on Heroes, he speaks of religion and the various types of worship, and quotes Plato's fancy about a man who grew to maturity in some dark, distant place and was brought all of a sudden into the upper air to see the sunrise. Imagine his rapt astonishment at a sight we witness daily with indifference. He would fall down in worship before it. One can visualise the sun-worshippers who still kept the wonder of the universe in their hearts.

'This world,' says Carlyle, 'after all our science and sciences, is still a miracle: wonderful, inscrutable, magical and more, to whoever will think of it.'

Bert has just returned from Dave's funeral. Rene, Doris and Ruby were there, and Elsie went back to Ballarat with them. At last she will be able to get away from Mannerim. What a relief it must be, for there isn't any doubt that this is a god-forsaken place.

11 May 1942

After an anxious time of waiting, at last a postcard came from Theo. Just a few lines. She is more neglectful in writing to me than any of the family. I do wish she would take five minutes to write more often. Five minutes is all that is necessary for a letter-card. A month's silence is too long.

Shaw is a tonic. The way he plays off the parents against the children and the children against the parents is simply magnificent. To be able to laugh at oneself is good. And he makes both sides do just that.

24 May 1942

I can hear guns in the distance. Horrid sound. It brings to one's mind all sorts of horrors.

Bill came home for part of the May holidays. He seems himself again. But never again shall I feel so poignantly about any of the children's doings. Although one cannot but be sorry rather than upset to see them interested in anyone second-class, so to speak. For Olwyn had lots of time to improve her mind, and material ready to hand, but one could see that chatter was her main occupation.

Of course, to see these things one must be in the home without the distraction of male attraction. If I had thought Bill was attracted, I should have told him many things said and done at Hamilton. The reason I didn't tell him there was that I wanted everything to go smoothly whilst I was with them.

30 October 1943

Herb home again: this time not to return to the battlefront. The trouble with his hands and feet has been successfully treated, but if he returned to the islands the callous condition would return. He is kept here on hospital duty and he is very annoyed at the part many are playing here. It is wicked, he says, to keep men in the front line for years while many who have joined up are kept here with weekends, holidays and a generally good time.

The long extended war is wearing to all, though the Allies must know what they are doing. The contrast between the German blitzing and the steady push of the Allies speaks for itself. For now the former are to see their conquests lost one by one in this steady drive towards our own objectives. We can see this in the Japanese drives too. This year it is significant that they didn't hold their usual Pearl Harbour celebrations. Now they have lost more than half their fleet and three quarters of their aircraft. Each day we hear of new successful assaults on their positions in the islands.

Hitler is being driven back, and out of Russia. In the last war, after several defeats, they cracked quite suddenly and when we heard the news of the surrender, everyone was thunderstruck, so sudden and unexpected it was.

After my illness in Geelong, where Dulcie nursed me with care and kindness, I do not seem to get strong. Perhaps I must content myself with the thought that old people tire anyway, illness or no illness.

Next month is the 50th Anniversary of our wedding, celebrated in Queenscliff on 29 November 1893. Life is as a dream. After all, fifty years is not long. As a girl of eighteen years, entering a life wholly unknown and untried, I was really afraid that day. In those years I have known anxiety, sickness, sorrow, the loss of all worldly goods by fire and much misery. Nevertheless, to offset that I have had much happiness in children, books, music and love.

My husband disappointed me because he made the seriousness of life his first consideration and work came before the children and home. If one was not working, time was wasted, even in listening to music or reading. I may have disappointed him too, and have often felt sorry that he had not chosen a woman more of his own kind.

That day fifty years ago

Ethel Thwaites married Herbert Fitzpatrick on 29 November 1893, at the new Wesleyan Church in Hesse Street, Queenscliff. Erected in 1888, the Victorian Gothic Revival church replaced the original small church, still standing next door. With building materials easily transported to Queenscliff by railway freight train, the red brick gabled and buttressed church designed by Melbourne architect T. J. Crouch had some attractive features.

A kauri pine barrel-vaulted ceiling led the eye to a beautiful rose kaleidoscope window above the altar, a backdrop to the ardent expression of the bride, keenly noted by Rev. John Adams. Adams officiated from the Drysdale Home Mission Circuit from which Queenscliff separated in 1899. The church floor was built on a slant to enhance the visibility and predominance of the preacher in the pulpit. Deconsecrated in 1981, when Methodists and Presbyterians combined as the Uniting Church, the former church opened as a restaurant in 2007.

12 December 1943

It was rather a moving experience, for me at least, to sit in Church at Queenscliff and go back in memory to that day fifty years ago, when as a girl of eighteen I promised so solemnly to 'honour and obey'. If one can't do the former, why the latter? The minister who performed the ceremony told my mother that he was impressed by the serious expression on my face, adding, 'She will keep her vow.' He did not know, nor did I, how hard that was to be, nor for how many years I strived to do so. But the law backs up the man anyhow and in many things the woman must 'obey' at least in the letter, no matter how the spirit rebels.

So if memories were sad, I had only to look at our family, as they stood in the Church that morning singing 'Dear Lord and Father of Mankind' for a deep glow of happiness to take its place.

It made me happy to know that Herb is safely home again and all that anxiety on that score is over. And Theo was home for a few days. She is so easy to live with, so even tempered, that it is a pleasure to have her about me. I only wish she were nearer.

And now Bill wants me to fly to Tasmania with him. I, who have never been able to endure heights. It makes me rather apprehensive, but I'll go.

Not a breath of romance filters through Ethel's diary pages, and it seems on the surface a marriage of convenience. 'Until recently it was marriage, rather than achievement, that determined a woman's rise in the world; women saw other women getting ahead on the basis of their beauty or sexuality. This old corruption of female meritocracy is compounded by the way the media today attributes women achievers' status to their looks or to a husband, male relative or male mentor.'[3] No doubt her parents, John and Mary Ann, believed she would be well taken care of and provided for by the conscientious baker Herbert Fitzpatrick. And indeed she was, as we see in his steady progress, with leasing multiple shops and property acquisitions in his borough rates payments.

She describes herself as poor, but growing up at Fishermen's Flat on the fringe of the comings and goings of the top echelons of Melbourne society fuelled Ethel Thwaites' ambition and expectation. She grew to harbour a deep resentment for the doors that closed upon marriage to a husband who was insensitive to her intellectual and social needs.

Chapter 11

Theo

Diverse WWII recreational and cultural pastimes for women

Women were involved in all manner of cultural and recreational pastimes during WWII. For example, in 1943 the composer Margaret Sutherland, close in age to Theo's eldest sister, with her musician friend Lorna Stirling showed amazing foresight with a vision of a cultural centre for the city of Melbourne. Sutherland wrote a letter to *The Age* calling for public support to transform the Wirth's Park Site into a centre for the arts. She recruited civil servant John Lloyd, who became president of the Combined Arts Centre Movement, with Sutherland as secretary.

> By June 1944, over seventeen petitions circulated. Sutherland and Stirling also held midday rehearsals to collect further signatures, for they believed: 'We just had to peg away'. Eventually they won. Over forty thousand signatures were collected in a petition to parliament for an Arts Centre on the Wirth's site. It took twelve years of campaigning until the site was made over to an Arts Centre by 'An Act providing for the establishment of The National Art Gallery and Cultural Centre Building Committee … in November 1956.' [1]

Despite debates during WWI over the propriety of continuing sporting activities during a national crisis, entertainment, recreation and sporting activities hardly missed a beat. It was considered that horse racing boosted morale, and football prepared for the serious business ahead. As for golf, the cost of trophies was donated to patriotic funds.[2]

And so it was in Tasmania during the Second World War, on a Good Friday morning in the mid-forties, despite rumours that the road was impassable with washaways, Theodora's expedition pressed on to Coles Bay, via Campbelltown, at 8.30am.

The drive beyond Lake Leake was through heavily timbered gum forests; and passing through Cranbrook the country was idyllically green, with especially beautiful dark-green wattles about, and brilliant splashes of yellow autumnal poplars. Beyond Cranbrook the road sweeps up a hill from which a delightful view is seen across the Bay of the Remarkables rising from the sea. Although the Remarkables are only about two thousand feet high, they present a most spectacular appearance.

On the arrival at the Sunshine Chalets we were directed to 'Bayside' and disposed of lunch before setting out on a walk to a nearby beach. The sand was East Tasmanian white sand, the sea was East Tasmanian peacock-blue sea and our beach curved away for over a mile to green-clad headlands of red rocks. The beach had a fascinating line of little breakers, very like those of Howrah, where the small waves swell up, to break with a diminutive, sharp 'crack!' Mona found an enormous shell fragment, which had whitened with age or sand-action. She and I walked to the very end of a beach, leaving Cecil and Mac drowsing on a sand-dune.

On the way back we had wonderful views of the Remarkables rising up from the sea about four miles away: it was rather the same sensation as standing on the sand on Dove Lake and looking towards Cradle Mountain. Here, however, sunlight glinted on the flying wings of seagulls out over the sea: they turned — and were invisible; and turned, and were again specks of silver in the sun, against purple hills. We all spent an hour or so searching for shells among the rock-pools at the end of the beach, a pastime of endless delight. At night there was a huge Easter moon illuminating the mountains and sea. Lights glowed across the water from the Chateau, the Fisheries and from stray fishing craft on the water. We were lulled to sleep by the soft sound of waves breaking gently on the rocks.

The lure of far horizons was upon us next day and we took the road to the Chateau on the opposite side of the bay from our chalets: a delightful sandy road through gum trees and low ti-tree in flower. The fragrant air — honey-sweet, salty and permeated with the subtle smell of eucalypts, was balm to us. Beyond the Chateau, the road proceeds through the heath. Ti-tree and gums overlook tiny bays where the water shines crystal-clear from the white sand bottom. The headlands of these miniature gem-like bays are red granite.

...

We had an efficient guide up to the Lookout, in a friendly great black dog, which had adopted us at the Chateau. While red granite is striking with its odd outlines, it is far more severe on the hands than dolerite rock. It is necessary for the walker to wear rubber-soled shoes on the surface of red granite, instead of the usual hob-nailed boots. Once on the Lookout, we saw Wineglass Bay below us — an alluring long white curve of beach demanding to be explored. Taking the track down, we lunched on biscuits and raisins, before walking to the far end of the bay. The breeze fanned us most beautifully with great limpid breakers rising to crash in white spray, seagulls gathering in conference on a section of beach, a school of porpoises playing in the bay and a penguin, who had chanced to call in, sitting beyond the breakers. At the far end of Wineglass Bay, where the sand was almost as white and fine as face-powder, we uncovered an almost buried fossil-bone, large enough to be the rib of a dinosaur or a whale.

On our return walk around Wineglass the aspect was altogether lovely: the Remarkables fell sheer to the sea, the sun glittered occasionally on wet rocks, beyond was the fading purple of the headlands, on the other side of the bay were orange and reddish hued rocks of the coastline and, bounded by the white curving beach, the sea was deep cobalt blue.

...

The next day found us oddly reluctant to dash out and view hills and beaches. We tried to get a boat, and failed, as they were all booked; we tried to think up super-easy walks, and couldn't. So we piled into the car and drove around to the Fisheries, calling on the Smithies where we found the respective members of the family, according to inclination, darning sandals, blowing iridescent soap bubbles from a special preparation, or paddling. We then set off for the Quarries and although active operations in the excavating of red granite ceased in August 1942, there were many tons of red granite blocks still awaiting shipment. The coastline appears to be composed of red granite and I for one would hate to be the master of a vessel attempting to approach the tiny pier at the Quarries during rough weather. Luckily, the East Coast is noted for its fine, mild climate.

At twelve noon we set off again to return to the car, and proceeded to Sleepy Bay, which is not the vast expanse of sand dunes you might imagine, but a rocky bay whose combination of red-orange cliffs and emerald green and clear deep blue sea is most satisfying. We passed the time lazily reading, sunbaking and watching crabs camouflaged with pink seaweed sidling about in a rock-pool. I ambled away to see what lay beyond the next headland, and was rewarded with the aspect of the sandy path winding on over the rounded hill, which was covered with bracken and the red heads of heath-bells and the rocky peaks of the mountains rising beyond.

We returned to the chalet for afternoon tea and a little later tried our luck at fishing. Mollymawks sat in imperturbable dignity upon the piles; immaculate gulls mewed beside us or wheeled about the pier; but the fish evidently had other business on hand as they didn't even flirt with the bait.

...

The following day was very wet, and confined to the chalet we read, knitted, yarned and indulged in continuous cups of tea. And the morrow, still wet, found us on the road home. Rain had brought the road to a sorry state and it was practically a chain of deep pools. However, from one point on the way we were rewarded with the sight of pelicans standing meditatively on a beach and further along were hundreds of black swans dotted upon the bay.

Some Reflections

Growing up on the Bellarine Peninsula, near Swan Bay, with great flocks of migrating birds sweeping along the shoreline and flying overhead in every sort of formation, gave Theodora Fitzpatrick a lifelong fascination with birds. Swans were plentiful ninety-five years ago, when many long, vee-shaped skeins could be seen drifting across the Bellarine skies at sunset. Easily becoming accustomed to people, and apparently vice versa, waterfowl such as Black Swans, which are now protected, found their way onto dinner tables in the pioneer days at Fishermen's Flat.

Some Reflections, a collection of Theo's verses, was published in Launceston to be gifted to family and friends, and includes a poem that examines a sleeping white swan:

Swan

From the ebon mirror of the pool,
Wrapped in the tranquil secrecy of night
With proud grace you glide into my sight.
I never have known beauty, never seen
Pureness of line, symmetry of form
To match your rich perfection: now you gleam
Motionless; and when, carved ivory you sleep,
What dreams does Beauty dream?

A window into Theo's Tasmanian wonderland

January 1945

The departure of the launch from Lake St Clair was like a scene from *Alice in Wonderland*. There were about nineteen people aboard, not to mention stores to be carried up to Pine Valley Hut; so about five of us, together with a 'possum in a bag', were given the grandstand position. It took ages to get going — first there was trouble in edging the launch away from the jetty, and then some difficulty cropped up with the engine.

However we eventually got away and nineteen people heaved a sigh of relief. There was a cold wind blowing, although the day was perfect. Turning for a last glimpse of the camp before rounding the bend in the lake, I blew a kiss to the beloved line of Mount Rufus rising to the sky in graceful beauty.

The mountains at the Northern end of the lake were wonderfully clear — the light had some peculiar clarity, which made them look enormous and impossible. Peak after peak rose — Olympus, Byron, Manfred, Pyramid Hill, The Guardians, the Gould Sugarloaf, Gould, the Acropolis, Cyrean, Falling, the Traveller's Range and Mount Ida. Mount Gould particularly dominated the landscape, raising its brown majestic head into the blue sky. And the day was so clear that we could see the needles of rock on top of the Acropolis.

After lunch at the Narcissus hut, the stores were removed from the launch and we trooped off up the track to Pine Valley, discovering a couple of echidnas along the way. My previous excursion to the Pine Valley hut had been accomplished in sleet and snow, and had resulted in a frost-bitten foot, without the reward of even a momentary glimpse of one mountain. But the perfection of this day annihilated the frustrations of the former trip; for today we saw the dark green pines of the valley, and each peak of the enclosing mountains. When we arrived at the hut the stores were dumped, and Ferg took us up through the green glades of the myrtle forest to see a very beautiful waterfall, tumbling in limpid waves over black rocks, some of which were partially covered in dark green moss.

Ferg and the St Clair party returned to the launch, leaving our party in possession of the hut. We sorted out our gear and argued happily as to which mountain we would climb on the morrow — Gould or Acropolis. There were no tracks beyond the hut, but Ferg had pointed out climbing lines for each. Sunset gave us a view of Gould against a golden sky and we had the pleasure of seeing the native cat, which Ferg had practically tamed when building the hut, being mercilessly teased by two or three mountain thrushes, in exactly the same way that minahs tease city cats.

Climbing Mount Gould

The weather was perfect when we set out to climb Mount Gould shortly after 9am. We walked down the valley to a huge dead gum tree, from where we proceeded upwards, towards the peaks of the Parthenon, turning at a sharp angle to the left, directly underneath the Parthenon cliffs and scrambling thence up to the Col. As there were no cairns on the mountain we made our way up to the summit; and there is no method of knowing exactly what is the summit, save that with a period of trial and error, climbing finally produces a spot from which the mountain appears lower.

We had an early lunch on the ridge between Gould and The Guardians, and then set out to walk all over the outer perimeter of the latter. We stood right at the cliff edge and gazed down to the clear waters of Lake Marion and walked and walked over the length of the mountain, finding several tarns filled with very large-sized Yanaspides. We gazed over towards Mount Cyrean and also along the wide, heavily timbered valley, which terminates in Mount Pelion West.

The next day Katie, Bill and I went up into the Labyrinth, a harmless-looking ridge from which has the most surprising and beautiful views across each of a chain of about three miles of lakes. The first lake is deep, and one side is fairly precipitous. There is a pencil pine or two and several flat-topped rocks, which invite the diver to leap into the water. The second lake is an idyll of beauty where, from a flat-rocked, heathered seat, we could see stands of pencil pines at the far end of the blue water, with a tiny white waterfall tumbling down the slope on the left and the needle pinnacles of the Acropolis and the precipices of Cyrean as a background to the whole scene.

The little lakes extend throughout the chain and there are infinite variations on the same theme of mountain-summit background with varied lake shapes, different outlines of pencil pines and heather-clad slopes. If I had to choose a parallel in music for the emotions aroused by the sight of Mount Gould the previous day it would be a Beethoven symphony, with Mozart's 'Divertimento 17' for the Labyrinth lakes!

Leaving the last lake we climbed over the rocks, up to the summit of Walled Mountain, where we lunched. From this vantage point, we surveyed the narrow but steep valley between the ridge and the Du Cane Range — the Acropolis, Cyrean, etc. We gazed longingly towards the apparently easy ridge terminating in Mount Eros as we disposed of our sandwiches and noted the quaint tarns of emerald green or sky-blue, lying at quite different levels on the Mount Eros ridge. After lunch we walked around our mountain, and never have I seen the pincushion plant so plentiful or flowering so profusely. We leaped from mound to mound, and some plants were enormous. No doubt we were rather heartless to tramp over the star-like flowers scattered on the green of the moss, but it is a delightfully resilient carpet.

The northern end of the mountain is interesting, where huge columns lie tilted at a steep angle, while many of their brothers have crashed to fragments, forming rock-falls extending far down into the green forests of the valley. Also at one point we found a strange little plateau where, if one sat down on a pincushion plant, only the tip of Eldon and Pelion West showed above its rim, while, standing up, the whole of these mountains and their attendant valleys and foothills are revealed. A tiny, clear streamlet flowed in a chain of pools across the pineapple grass and moss, as if Nature, for the fun of it, had made a parody of the Labyrinth!

On the way home we swam in one of the lakes: swimming is a courtesy term, for after the first paralytic shock one is not fully conscious until returning to dry land. Mists enveloped us on the climb down, and we were very glad to reach the hut and the food awaiting us. For the next two days the weather played all its worst tricks, and even on the third, the day of departure, we were rained upon in the early part of the walk back to the Narcissus Hut.

Fergie was to have met us here with the launch, but at 8 o'clock he had not put in an appearance, so Katie and I decided to walk the fifteen miles to the Camp, and rather than follow the myrtle-forest track, we took the track over the Byron Saddle. We made very good walking time, and the view from the Saddle was superb. Looking back across the Narcissus

River were the mountains amongst which we had spent the last few days, and turning to follow the track we saw the clear outline of Frenchman's Cap between a frame of hills. The track passes around the beautiful Lake Petrach. From one beach of this, between pencil pines, we had a view of Mount Byron, wreathed in gossamer mists. On goes the track, down the golden button-grass of Cuvier Valley, and although where we walked there was very little wind, there was a gale blowing on Mount Olympus' peaks and the valley was filled with this ominous sound.

Queenscliff Pier. Rich gold diggers travelled to Queenscliff for holidays in the 1860s, followed by an influx of the Melbourne gentry in the 1880s. It became 'the fashionable place' to stay or visit. *Photo courtesy of the Queenscliffe Historical Museum*

Paddle Steamer *Weeroona* at Queenscliff Pier. With steamers travelling from Melbourne to Queenscliff in under two hours, and many services between Melbourne, Geelong, Sorrento and Queenscliff, Queenscliff had around 50,000 visitors a year. The large waiting shed for the ladies was constructed on the pier in 1887. *Photo courtesy of the Queenscliffe Historical Museum*

Queenscliff lifeboat practice. A lifeboat service was needed at the entrance to Port Phillip Bay due to the treacherous waters there, known as 'The Rip' or 'The Heads'. The service was established in 1858, utilising the crew of the Health Officer's boat. In the 1890s, the responsibility passed to the local fishermen. *Photo courtesy of the Queenscliffe Historical Museum*

Queenscliff fishing fleet. The first commercial fishermen came to Queenscliff around 1860. They camped on the sand flats near their boats and Queenscliff's first jetty. Complaints about this 'squatting' led to allotments being surveyed and leased to licensed fishermen and their families. This area became known as Fisherman's Flats, a distinctive part of Queenscliff, recalling the importance of the fishing industry in the town's development. In 1891, the Marine Disaster Bell, which was rung to summon the volunteer lifeboat crew, was installed. *Photo courtesy of the Queenscliffe Historical Museum*

Thwaites Walk, seen from the Queenscliff Lighthouse, was named as a mark of respect for all the men of the pioneer Thwaites family. This included a prominent Lord Mayor, fishermen, boatmen, seamen and long-serving members of the volunteer lifeboat crews. Ironically, it became a promenade for the top echelons of Victorian society during the late nineteenth century and early twentieth century, and it was here that the gap between locals and the affluent was most apparent. *Photo courtesy of the Queenscliffe Historical Museum*

The Sea Baths were located between the Queenscliff pier and the Sea Pilots Jetty. The white pilot vessel *Alvina* is shown on a return trip. They provided safe, segregated hot and cold bathing facilities from 1891 to 1934. Unfortunate destruction of native flora occurred when the timber from the surrounding area provided fuel for heating the hot sea baths. *Photo courtesy of the Queenscliffe Historical Museum*

Dr Alexander Robertson, one of the earliest Queenscliff medical officers, in a gig outside his pre-1860 timber residence. Here was the orchard where he set a trap to catch Ethel Thwaites' schoolboy brother William, the future mayor of Queenscliff, pilfering his fruit. Next door his assistant, Dr David Williams, built the 1860s house he leased to Dr Richardson, whose daughter was Henry Handel Richardson.
Photo courtesy of the Queenscliffe Historical Museum

Common School No. 516. This weatherboard hall, originally on the corner of Hobson and Learmonth Street from 1862 to 1873, downhill from St George the Martyr Church of England, was first used in 1854 as the Anglican Sunday School. School master Robert Jordan and assistant Miss Green are standing on the steps.
Photo courtesy of the Queenscliffe Historical Museum

The Grand Hotel on Hesse Street, Queenscliff, Easter Parade Artillery Band in 1883. This was the largest and most extravagant hotel in Queenscliff. It had the same architect as the Windsor Hotel in Melbourne. Photograph by Frederick Kruger. *Photo courtesy of the Queenscliffe Historical Museum*

Hesse Street business of William John Thwaites, 1868 to 1929. William, son of John and Mary Ann Thwaites, standing outside with some of his ten children, possibly during his first term as mayor in 1910. He is probably holding the hand of five-year-old Dorothy, with wife Amy. Their toddler and baby are not pictured. *Photo courtesy of the Queenscliffe Historical Museum*

Herbert Fitzpatrick and Ethel Fitzpatrick (nee Thwaites), 29 November 1893. *Photo from Theo's collection, courtesy of Lorraine Secen*

Ethel Fitzpatrick (nee Thwaites) 1875–1958. *Photo from Theo's collection, courtesy of Lorraine Secen*

Theodora Fitzpatrick cycling along the road to New Norfolk, on the Derwent River, in south-east Tasmania. *Photo from Theo's collection, courtesy of Lorraine Secen*

Theo on the Lachlan Track, November 1941. *Photo from Theo's collection, courtesy of Lorraine Secen*

Timber mill at the foot of Higgs' Track to Chudleigh Lakes, Tasmania. Photo stamped 'F. Smithies 34 Paterson Street, Launceston'. *Photo from Theo's collection, courtesy of Lorraine Secen*

Some of the Launceston Walking Club. Theo is the second from the left. Photo attributed to F. Smithies. *Photo from Theo's collection, courtesy of Lorraine Secen*

Summer trip to Summit Hut, Ben Lomond. Theo is seated on the right. This unsigned photo is attributed to Smithies because on the same day a photo was taken in which Theo appears in the same clothes, which has pencilled on the back 'Summit Hut, Ben Lomond, Summer Trip' and is signed by F. Smithies. *Photo from Theo's collection, courtesy of Lorraine Secen*

Theo, second on the left, passing the Pool of Siloam. It was a challenging walk through a remote area of Tasmania to the The Walls of Jerusalem. Photo stamped 'F. Smithies'. *Photo from Theo's collection, courtesy of Lorraine Secen*

Theodora's Tarn, with Theo seated in the centre. Photo stamped 'F. Smithies'. *Photo from Theo's collection, courtesy of Lorraine Secen*

Interior of Tent, 1921. *Photo courtesy of the Tasmanian Archive and Heritage Office. NS 573-4-4-51.tif from NS 573, AOT 2005 Tasmania State Library*

Three female bushwalkers wearing 'putties' on tea break, Cradle Mountain, 1925 or 1926. *Photo courtesy of the Tasmanian Archive and Heritage Office. NS 573-4-9-21.tif from NS 573, AOT 2005 Tasmania State Library*

Six bushwalkers climbing Mount Ossa, Tasmania in 1921, with female bushwalkers wearing skirts and restrictive corsets. *Photo courtesy of the Tasmanian Archive and Heritage Office. NS 573-4-4-46.tif from NS 573-4-9-21 Tasmania State Library*

Ascending Frenchmen's Cap from Lake Tahune. Photo signed by F. Smithies. *Photo from Theo's collection, courtesy of Lorraine Secen*

Theo and companion near the pinnacle of Cradle Mountain, with Lake Rodway below. Photo attributed to Smithies as it is his style of composition, and the paper and printing are identical to his other photos. *Photo from Theo's collection, courtesy of Lorraine Secen*

Theo and companion near the pinnacle of Cradle Mountain. Photo attributed to Smithies as it is his style of composition, and the paper and printing are identical to his other photos. *Photo from Theo's collection, courtesy of Lorraine Secen*

Theo at Whymper Crags, Ben Lomond, October 1947. Photo signed by F. Smithies. *Photo from Theo's collection, courtesy of Lorraine Secen*

Launceston at Cataract Gorge. Photo signed by F. Smithies. *Photo from Theo's collection, courtesy of Lorraine Secen*

Waldheim Chalet under snow. *Photo courtesy of the Tasmanian Archive and Heritage Office. NS 573-4-12-128.tif from NS 573-4-9-21, Tasmania State Library*

Snow bound cars at Great Lakes. *Photo courtesy of the Tasmanian Archive and Heritage Office. NS 573-4-8-9.tif from Tasmania State Library*

Taking provisions to Summit Hut, winter trip, 1943. Photo signed by F. Smithies. *Photo from Theo's collection, courtesy of Lorraine Secen*

Theo skiing at the Summit Hut, Ben Lomond, 1943 Taken at the same time as the previous photo, on the same paper and printing as Smithies' work, with his distinctive style of composition. Photo attributed to F. Smithies. *Photo from Theo's collection, courtesy of Lorraine Secen*

Chalet, Ben Lomond, 4000'. Photo signed by F. Smithies. *Photo from Theo's collection, courtesy of Lorraine Secen*

Theo on deck, sailing to Europe on the *Orion*, May 1948. Photo owned by Theo. *Photo from Theo's collection, courtesy of Lorraine Secen*

Ethel and Mannerim farm cat, Liebchen, 1948. Photo owned by Theo. *Photo from Theo's collection, courtesy of Lorraine Secen*

Christine Westhorpe Fitzpatrick, Theo's Scottish paternal grandmother. This photo, discovered following her stay in Scotland, was Theo's treasured keepsake. *Photo from Theo's collection, courtesy of Lorraine Secen*

Chapter 12

Ethel

Economic independence for all women

Jean Daley was among feminists who proclaimed throughout the 1920s and 1930s that all women regardless of class, marital status or race should enjoy economic independence.

> Mothers should raise their daughters to be self-supporting, she advised in her column in Woman's Clarion in 1925, for women who depended on men 'moulded themselves to his desire'.[1]

After raising seven children in a shop dwelling with her baker husband, the more cultured wife, Ethel, was stranded and unfulfilled in the isolation of their semi-retirement to a Mannerim farm. She was almost seventy by the time they had all left home, including Theo, who she had when she was forty. We can see in the tone of her prolific letters how jealously she guarded her relationship with her two youngest, unmarried children.

It is well documented that 'many young women, growing up as witnesses to their mothers' lives in the Depression, were determined not to live as they did. The memory of the drudgery and unhappiness weighed heavily'.[2] The same could be said for young men, but in bachelor Bill's case one wonders whether the predictable Ethel was merely a convenient scapegoat for a son who was shy of marital responsibility.

Muriel had a man in her room

Ethel's diary is frequently the repository for personal matters, and the writing keeps her on an even keel. She wrote two versions of a domestic altercation from her Launceston stay, giving a more detailed account upon her return to Mannerim. One always suspects that the blame lies somewhere in the middle with such things, and perhaps Ethel wanted to whitewash her part in triggering Muriel's extreme behaviour.

14 January 1944

Muriel was so peculiar as to defy description. Her lecture to me on manners was one of the funniest things really. It was the result of a call at the door for me, which she answered. Instead of leaving me to conduct my own affairs, she stood there while the man from the bureau told me, 'You will be disappointed I'm afraid, Mrs Fitzpatrick, in your trip to Mount Barrow.'

'How's that?' I asked, since he'd given no reason.

'Well that's a long story,' he replied.

'Well there must be a reason. Is the trip cancelled?'

'No.'

'Is it that you can take two people instead of one, myself?'

'No. I'm sorry for the disappointment. Would you like to go to Lavender Farm on Sunday?'

'No, thank you,' I said. 'I like to make my own arrangements and I find your excuses ridiculous, to say the least.' I walked away, leaving Muriel standing there.

She followed me inside and, among other things, told me I was rude. 'The trouble with you,' she said, 'is you've no God and no-one to help you.'

The reason for the cancellation was something quite different. I worked it out as a bit of personal spite. Muriel had a man in her room the whole of one evening. Getting up the next morning I noticed the door into the lounge leading into the hall outside was open and I closed it. She flew into a rage, and said it was no good trying to sleep here and was off to the seaside. Anyone with half an eye could see she was mad because she had let him out that way and didn't close it for fear of us knowing. The unknown man is the driver on the mountain trips and together they instigated the little plot to cause me disappointment. So, at least Theo thinks.

15 January 1944

Madge came back from the trip yesterday giving us news of Bill, who has to go slow on the return journey to help Gwladys, who has sprained her ankle. Poor Gwladys! Poor Bill! All the same, he couldn't possibly desert her. It all fits in with the other numerous mishaps on this tour. He will be amused at affairs here when he arrives.

18 January 1944

I am looking forward to Bill's return and hope he will not be disappointed with his trip, tho' that could hardly be. At the most it will mean that with Gwladys's sprained foot, they must go slower. Madge came back very enthusiastic about Cradle Mountain. There were quite a number of people in the group and all were thrilled with the marvellous views, and finding snow still on the plateau to frolic around.

Theo will never return to Mannerim

Ethel's 'breakpoint' was painful for the family. The adult children and their spouses watched while their mother and mother-in-law struggled with the isolation of Mannerim. The constant son, high school teacher Bill, shouldered much of the burden. Retirement brought neither release nor joy for the Fitzpatrick couple. Without grandchildren to focus on they had little in common. We feel all the while that Ethel, and perhaps all the family, is waiting for magic to happen when Theo marries. She had reached the stage where, as Melissa Benn wrote, 'Confidence is buoyed by experience but an inner stubbornness has grown too, a refusal always to keep the peace, keep the job, keep the goodwill of the more powerful.'[3]

12 February 1944

My time had been filled with writing and gazing at the changing scene out of the window. It is so very beautiful here. Immediately below is the very pretty, laid-out flowerbeds with bricks crossing each other between them. On one side are broad and low steps in a semi-circle leading to a swimming pool. On the other side is a gently sloping brick path, also leading to the pool and meeting the steps at a gate leading to the pool. Three steps down and you are on a path leading to dressing sheds, on one side a raised grass plot and on the other a platform with big ferns and a seat running along its length. The pool itself is seven feet deep at one end and four foot at the other. Shrubs line the steps leading down to a pool, and on each side of the dressing sheds is a statue: such a pretty spot.

Beyond the pool are trees, behind them are big houses and beyond those are the beautiful tall trees of a park and beyond again and around it lies the town, the red roofs of which with the river winding in and out among them, and the hills and mountains beyond that again, is a most beautiful view. Everyone that comes here is in love with it. It is really an expensive flat with its five rooms, a bathroom, long, long sunroom, lounge, large bedroom, small bedroom, breakfast room and kitchen: six rooms counting the sunroom, which is huge, running the length of the house.

Theo will never return to Mannerim: she has gotten far from there with its circumscribed atmosphere. Everyone here speaks so highly of her that I'm often quite embarrassed. Mr Kinmott, the Head of the Tasmanian branch of Chartres, told me he knows of no other woman who could do the job she is doing, also that her personality is an asset to any firm lucky enough to get her services. He said it would be impossible to speak too highly of her.

I am hating to leave all of this. For one thing the work is clean and light and I'm feeling A1, except that I cannot negotiate these streets, they are so terribly steep. But there's no need to go out, really. One can see all over the town, which is spread out far beneath us and indeed, away beyond it. Just opposite is a park, with a view of three big mountains,

Mount Arthur, Barrow and Ben Lomond, where Theo has gone today, returning tomorrow evening. Then on Monday morning, at 8am, I leave for Hobart again.

14 February 1944

Went to Hobart by bus and was welcomed with open arms by Gwladys. She wasn't expecting me, and was surprised and delighted when the maid knocked at her door and told her of my arrival. She came hurrying in to greet me and explained that she was at the gate waiting to welcome me, saw the bus sail by and went inside. Neither she nor I knew there were two buses that morning and I was on the second one. There was a bit of a mix up, too, when the driver didn't know where 45 Main Road was. It appears that two years ago, the name was changed to Newtown Road. Luckily, a lady on the bus knew where Theo used to live and I was put down right on the doorstep.

Poppa Morris, too, was glad to see Theo's mother. He was amused at there being three Ethels there on the same day. He's a nice old man, but failing fast and a great responsibility for Gwladys.

My hand looms large on the paper

So much of the communication between mother and daughter, Ethel and Theodora, relied on the written word in the form of letters. Would the relationship have been different with the advantages of the twenty-first century, and the unprecedented image and text message opportunities of this age? It would depend on how Ethel adjusted to using the language of the digital age, captured cleverly here by Melissa Benn:

> And how much less lovely it sounds too, the descriptors themselves so much shorter, sharper, more brisk; thrusting rather than reflective. This shift in, and shortening of, language reflects a sea change in thinking between the generations too.[4]

In the anonymous mix of social media platforms such as Twitter, people of all ages contribute to a common forum on a scale unprecedented in the history of the world. Twitter is intolerant of bullying, and you'll see that a transparent, open-ended taunt like, 'Chick's feathers ruffled by sixty-something warrior woman!' will dissipate like a ripple in the ocean. However, in 1944, computers, the internet and mobile phones didn't exist, and written communication was strictly by snail mail or the dreaded telegram:

17 April 1944

News came today of Alice's death yesterday. No details in telegram. I would like so much to go up, but can't go to Melbourne alone now, because it confuses me. I must get Bert to send a telegram and will write also. One after the other the family are passing. That makes five gone (Nellie, Alf, Jim, Will, Alice). Who will be next?

7 July 1944

Dearest Theodora,

I write all my letters lately sitting in my own light, with the pad on my knee. Because I can't be far from the fire, the light is behind me and the shadow of my hand looms large on the paper.

I hope the floods around Launceston are not very bad this year. Pop read the reports about it to me this evening and wanted to know where the South Esk is. Does the view from your sunroom show you the flooded area? I often think of that view. It is really lovely.

I'm terribly sorry to hear about your dental sorrows and sympathise with you. I truly believe that it is the wisest thing to have them all out. Jean Mac's teeth are beautiful. Nowadays a good dentist can work miracles. There's a Dr Newman in Geelong who specialises in girls' teeth and just imagine, no more misery!

How's the knee? You didn't mention it in your last letter. Perhaps the present trouble overshadowed the memory of the knee, just as your — well righteous indignation did, when you were left to 'carry the baby'.

I have been reading a book of essays Bill gave me some time ago. There are several word pictures of various authors that are most interesting and particularly, I think, that of Gibbon, the author of *The Rise and Fall of the Roman Empire*. Here is a concentrated description:

> A little figure, extraordinarily rotund surmounted by a top-heavy head, with a button nose planted amid a vast expanse of cheek and ear, and chin upon chin rolling downward. Nor was this appearance only: the odd shape reflected something of the inner man. Mr Gibbon was always slightly overdressed. He was a little vain, a little pompous: at the first moment one almost laughed: and then one forgot everything under the fascination of that even flow of admirably intelligent, exquisitely turned and most amusing sentences. The astonishing creature was able to make a virtue even of absurdity. Without that touch of nature he would have run the risk of being too much of a good thing. As it was, there was no such danger: he was preposterous and a human being.

You will guess of course that the essayist is Strachy. He describes Gibbon as a happy being: happiness being the word that immediately rises to the mind at the thought of him. Every happening in his life came at the right moment. Even his disappointments were blessings in disguise.

But, I *must* stop and finish the sleeve of my jumper.

Lots of love. Look after your face.

Mother

Rearing children in a cake and sweets shop

Much of Ethel Fitzpatrick's 1940s restlessness and frustration can be viewed in the context of the groundswell of women wanting more than economic independence for all women. This wasn't going to happen overnight. Melissa Benn was referring to the 1960s and 1970s when she said, 'here were women wanting things, sex, money, fame, power — and wanting them just for themselves, not for the health of society or in the name of the collective good.'[5] For Ethel, rearing children in a Queenscliff cake and sweets shop, it was still so far away.

31 July 1944

Sixty-nine today! In reality beginning the 70th year of life, the allotted span. I lay in bed this morning looking back on life, as I suppose most people do on their birthdays. I'm quite certain of one thing. Knowing the past, I could not face the same again: the constant struggle, not so much against circumstances, but against Bert in every way. I should have enjoyed the children and the home life, for they were intelligent and healthy, except when obliged to work too hard on improper food, for a cake and sweets shop is by no means a good place in which to rear children.

18 August 1944

Dearest Theo,

Are you really and honestly thinking of coming over here? Why not take a couple of months, good solid rest at home among the books and general restfulness. Wouldn't it tempt you to let your rotten machines wait on themselves or rust to the devil?

13 February 1945

Dear Theodora,

I wrote you a silly letter the other day because I thought you needed something of the sort. I know you are disappointed at being tied over there. By this time you should be getting used to the struggle of getting away from anywhere. So far as I can remember it has always been the same. With this difference — this time of war blocks you as so many others. But there are indications that it won't last much longer, don't you think?

I'm a bit worried about you dear. Bessie tells me that you are losing weight and that, in conjunction with knee trouble and conking out in the mountains, makes me think that you should see a doctor. I don't want to frighten you, but tuberculosis is stalking around and in a cold climate it just luxuriates. I have just been reading 'Leaves from a surgeon's notebook'. He insists that everyone should be tested for that complaint as so many have it without their having the slightest inkling. It wouldn't do any harm to see a doctor now and again.

Dad made six-dozen tarts today, for the Red Cross people, who are enterprising enough to serve afternoon tea in a marquee. It ought to bring them a bit of money. Lennie is giving bread rolls and hot dogs. All the women are doing something. The catch is the sugar hold up. Although the men returned to work yesterday it will be some time before we get our due rations and I can assure you that it is pretty difficult trying to stretch our reduced rations.

I have just read a screamingly funny story about 'a fool dog'. It is about a homemade bomb that was to be used as a detonation for blasting rocks on the banks of a creek in the search for gold. Three miners in their spare time fished in the creek and one day one of them concocted the idea of using a small bomb instead of the fishing line method.

The bomb being ready, it was stood against the pole of the tent to harden the water resisting stuff. The miners were grouped around the open fire waiting for dinner, with their backs to the tent, when they saw their mate plonk down the plate of chops and go for his life. One of the others saw him and he too ran like the devil. The third miner gaped at the other two, who never looked around, but kept yelling, 'Run, run.' But when he did look around, he saw what had happened.

The fool dog had the bomb in his mouth and was tearing around, shaking and growling. So the third man joined the others, or tried to. Puppy made after them, but this time with the tube hissing like mad. They all ran into a hotel in a nearby village and told them what was happening. There was such a stampede for the door that they got jammed, cursing one another and, principally, the men who owned the dog.

When they got out they knew they couldn't get anywhere far enough to be safe, so they ran into a wash house at the back of the hotel which was on a foundation three feet from the ground. By this time the bomb was near to explosion and as they watched from the window they saw the fool dog run under it, to be instantly chased out by a yellow mongrel whose special quarters it was.

In the paddock next door the mongrel bit the fool dog, which dropped the bomb as he hurtled thro' the fence. The yellow mongrel turned to go home when he remembered that the funny looking thing might be good to eat. All he did was grab it when a great bang shook the district, lifting the washhouse off its piles and gently back again. All that was left of the yellow dog was a few tufts of hair sticking to the shattered fence pickets. There were many limping dogs in the district afterwards, but the fool dog wasn't hurt a bit and went home wagging his tail and gambolling around as if pleased with the whole business.

All this doesn't sound nearly as funny as the book, but I was delighted with the fine Henry Lawson style. Dorothy wants me to go to Bendigo. She has the house to herself as the owners are going away for a holiday. I can't go because I'm just getting well again and I want to bottle some fruit Bill got for me. Sorry for that too, not the fruit, but having to turn down a change of scenery. Dad sends his love and says that you are not to bother about cigars for him. Enclosing a bit of wool I'm to make up for you when I see a nice pattern. I've nearly finished a little white one in an unusual style from the latest Paton book.

Ethel battling a head wind

The news of Henry Handel Richardson's death, in England in 1946 after an eighteen-month battle with cancer, isn't recorded in Ethel's diary and nor is she ever mentioned by name. Had the passing of the former Ethel Richardson of Queenscliff filtered through to Australia? Possibly not.

> A common complaint was that Australia had no 'spiritual life'. They were 'not cultured' — Sydney did not even have an opera house and few people went to concerts. No one told them about Henry Handel Richardson, Australia's famous writer, whose best

> novel, Maurice Guest (1908), is about the lives of music students in Leipzig, where Richardson herself had studied.[6]

Nevertheless, these two Ethels shared a deep love of music and literature. Both Ethels were passionate about characterisation in novels, which each of them referred to as 'character drawing'.

27 March 1946

I'm trying to pluck up the courage to battle with a head wind. Mrs Harding has been sick for some time and I feel I should make an effort to see her. Bert of course is much too busy to take me in the jinker; this wonderful farm takes a tremendous amount of waste time. Well perhaps not *waste* time because it is filling it up really until death comes and it *can't* be far off.

In looking back through life I'm amazed that he has never looked a fact in the face. He runs past it and round it, and if he has to look that way at all, it is out of the corner of his eyes. *Then* he loses his temper and blames everyone but himself. Naturally, the pleasant facts of life are all *his* making, and he is perfectly self-satisfied. But when unpleasant facts *should* be faced, the result is temper, glooming, exasperation and general misery in the sweet, sweet home.

Bill doesn't know what really decided me to take the trip in an aeroplane. I was terribly nervous at first, but when I considered my home life, the risk of accident couldn't be compared with it. The same applied to the Mount Barrow excursion. When I looked at that high zigzag path above me, the same thought sustained. If we fell, it was sure death, might be nasty, but soon over. Instead, the alternative of a lingering miserable life isn't attractive.

I suppose Bert's happy: in the true Irish fashion there must be a grievance. That old saying 'tritt arf the taal o'me coat' is very true. The significance of that saying, in interpretation, is of course that no-one was treading on his coat, but he *wants* a reason. The quarrel every Irishman goes about looking for. If he can have it at home, all the better.

Unblinking round eyes like Liebie

Theo had minimal parental interference in her personal affairs, with her ageing mother making just one trip to Tasmania. But bachelor Bill was not so lucky. With Gwladys Morris in his sights, or vice versa, while Bill's mother was staying with Theo in Launceston in January 1944, he returned to work and the enterprising Gwladys invited Ethel to stay with her family in Hobart. One suspects from Ethel's diary that the attraction was one-sided, that she either didn't feel threatened by Gwladys or that the kind offer of hospitality was accepted on face value as coming from Theo's friend, rather than Bill's.

It was a different story two years later, when Bill's romance with Dorothy, off to a promising start in the summer of 1945, came seriously unstuck with his mother in the spring of 1946.

30 April 1946
Dear little Daughter,

We had the admirable Dorothy here this weekend. All smirks and smiles and very correct speech as if she is speaking to a class. She's got unblinking round eyes like Liebie when she's guarding her kittens.

15 September 1946
Dearest Theo,

Some walkers — three men stopped to speak to me as I sat in the car at Queenscliff. They told me they were going to Tasmania for Christmas and asked me if I knew anything about it. I told them my daughter was over there and loved the mountains. I suggested a car to take them near the mountains, but they said they were taking bikes with them.

I told you that Bill took me to the Grampians with Dulcie and Dorothy. It was lovely, except for that fool of a Dorothy. She has a habit of roaring laughter at every little thing. One day I was sitting in the sun and she came out and saw me. 'Oh, she's sitting in the sun,' she said, roaring laughter. I said very quietly, 'It *may* be funny, but I'm damned if I can see it.' She *did* look a fool for about a minute. Bill seems to think she is wonderful for some reason I can't see.

Still I wish he wasn't such an ass over Dorothy. I dislike her for running after him from room to room, and looking so innocently and sweetly up into his face. I could cut her throat.

Pop is back from church and is talking like a gramophone. So I think I'll close.

Chapter 13
Theodora, Nancy and Rosaline
There were women on the peaks!

Society in general, educated with patriarchal history books that perpetuated marriage as the goal of all women, might be forgiven for feeling pity or scorn for the three spinsters Theo, Nancy and Steve, who climbed the formidable Frenchman's Cap in the late autumn of 1944, without a male in tow. In fact, the female trio who climbed Frenchman's Cap were exceptional and inspirational women of their generation. They carried the flag for women during the 1940s, keeping a foot in a door that was barely open to women and all too ready to be slammed shut. Theodora Fitzpatrick and her companions made it normal for women to explore the Tasmanian wilderness, walk the Overland Track, ski and hike in sensible clothing, take day jobs to pay for tertiary night lectures, qualify as accountants, undertake successful and rewarding careers, finance overseas trips, and submit and write about those experiences for publication.

Recognition of Rosaline Stephensen

With the photos of women's 1930s and 1940s wilderness pursuits omitted from the Smithies Collection in the Tasmanian Archives, and with publishers in the mid-1940s keeping the lid on the activities of progressive women by rejecting Theo's book about women's outdoor recreation in Tasmania, there was a very real possibility of the women of the future losing some significant role models.

However, in 1993 the National Museum of Australia's People and the Environment section travelled to Queensland to interview Rosaline

Stephensen (Steve), one of the trio involved in Theo's 1944 climb of Frenchman's Cap. Steve maintained a regular correspondence with Theo. The friendship forged in the Tasmanian wilderness endured, even though the three women lived in different states. There were warm letters such as this one, written by Steve on 24 January 1984, from Labrador, Queensland:

> One of my nieces has recently embarked on a trip to Franklin River. She is young and enthusiastic. I did not get to the area she hopes to explore, but I did encounter the Franklin and its fallen tree crossings on the way to Frenchman's Cap. You were with me on one trip. They were happy times, weren't they? I still correspond with a few people from those halcyon days. I haven't done much bushwalking over the last couple of years, but at least the ranges are in my sight.

Steve wrote from Biggera Waters, in her native Queensland, on November 1993:

> The years go by and all bring surprises. The real surprise for me began in October 1992 when I received a request from the National Museum in Canberra. The project was 'How women have changed in what used to be male dominated outdoor sports and interests from 1920 to 1950 — such as bushwalking and skiing'. I lived in Tasmania for thirty-one years and for most of the time I was an active member of the Hobart Walking Club.
>
> I came back to Queensland in 1966 and fortunately brought with me some souvenirs, such as an article of the four of us climbing Mount Anne. The mountains in Tasmania are superb; it's not their height, but their character. I gave the researcher, Sarah Waight, as much information as I could, including my opinion that Walking Club males are not dominant, but as members get to know each other, it grows into fellowship. Mrs Waight came to Queensland to interview me, recorded what I had to say on cassette tapes and now I have a copy.

In 1993, Sarah Waight interviewed Rosaline Stephensen, who was among the first women to challenge the dominance of men in the outdoor pursuits of bushwalking, skiing and mountaineering in Australia. Like Theo, Steve was a qualified accountant. She joined the Hobart Walking Club prior to 1935, when meetings were held in Jessie Luckman's music studio. Steve claimed that having a mother who was broadminded and didn't object to her camping out with the opposite sex was a definite advantage.

Equipment was a constant subject of conversation, she told Sarah Waight. Everyone told everyone else if they found something new, she said. Around 1935 and 1936, Steve wore gaiters made from whalebone to keep them up, and she had a good eider sleeping bag that lasted for years. Second-hand gear could be bought, but she saved up and bought good-quality equipment from Paddy Pallin. When she went camping she weighed every scrap of food and clothing that went into her pack so it would not weigh more than around thirty kilograms, and even tried to get it down to under twenty kilograms. She always carried a small axe, but never a tent.

Steve mentioned that Mount Wellington was easy walking and the place most people went. They also went over the back of Mount Wellington, she said, which was a much harder walk. Further afield on longer trips, Mount Wellington was a good place to start skiing, but Mount Field, where there was a university clubhouse, was better. Getting skis was a business in Hobart, and care had to be taken what timber the skis were made from. Leo Luckman had a lot of information on skiing equipment.

Steve helped with the building of a shelter shed on Mount Wellington, known as Luckman's Hut, with Leo Luckman, a stonemason. She also participated in the building of a cabin at Lake Dobson, in memory of three club members who died during the war, including her youngest brother.

Mount Anne stood out in her mind as being a memorable place, especially for its beauty and vegetation. Lake Pedder was also a beautiful and unique place: 'They had a nerve to call the place Lake Pedder after flooding. We slept on the beach of Lake Pedder. It had a special aura.'

Surprisingly, Rosaline Stephensen's insightful 1939 *Walkabout* magazine feature story, 'Mount Anne and the Port Davey Track', with photos by Leo Luckman, isn't mentioned in Waight's interview. This is unfortunate, as it was quite likely her sole publication.

All the trips were entertaining, records the National Museum of Australia. A Hungarian club member would beat his chest. People played up, but it was all part of the life of the club. Rosaline gave up walking around the start of the 1990s. She told Waight that her last trip was when she was staying with cousins in Nambour, and had tried unsuccessfully to get them to accompany her to the Glasshouse Mountains, as she wouldn't climb on her own. Desperate to go, she found a scout troop who agreed to let her tag along, but they were too slow. When she reached the top she could see the scouts loitering below.[1]

Communicating with the dead

On 2 February 2005, I was copying Theo's account of the Easter hike to Frenchman's Cap onto my laptop. When I got to the part where the three women were climbing a mountain where ancient glaciers had carved Tasmania's highest cliff out of white quartzite rock, where the weather was deteriorating and the intrepid mountaineers were in trouble, I took a break. Theo's address book was open beside me, with Nancy Shaw's phone number listed. I believed that all three women had passed away, but on the off-chance of finding someone who'd known Nancy, I dialled her number.

The clear, strong voice of 95-year-old Nancy Shaw announced herself and shock took my breath away. Not only that, the temperature in Melbourne — a sweltering thirty-six degrees — began to drop freakishly and rain suddenly bucketed down. With 50 millimetres of rain falling from midnight, more than our February average of 46.8 millimetres, not only did we have the wettest February day since 1998, we shivered through the coldest February day on record.

I was speaking in person to one of the women who'd climbed Frenchman's Cap sixty years earlier, when moments before I'd believed all the participants were dead. I told her I was writing a book about their exploits.

'Oh,' she said dubiously. 'Are you a Tasmanian?'

I knew why she was checking my credentials. No doubt, like Theodora Fitzpatrick, she deplored those who wrote books about Tasmania after the most slender acquaintance. Theo's account of hiking and skiing in the Tasmanian wilderness in the early 1940s carried a passionately Taswegian imprimatur that was bluntly dismissive of interlopers:

> This book was written as an answer from Tasmania to those written about the island by visitors. From one who has spent years exploring the infinite variety and scenic beauty of Tasmania, while some recorded trips are brief and incomplete, I hope that they reflect the spirit of delight and comradeship fostered by the mountains.

On 19 March 2005, Lorraine Secen and I flew to Tasmania to meet Nancy Weaver, the former Nancy Shaw, who was still living independently in her Hobart apartment.

'I think my generation had the best of things,' Nancy began. 'The bush, for instance.'

'You were saying that when you walked it was to escape from an oppressive family,' commented Lorraine. 'Looking back to the 1930s and 1940s — what gumption you had!'

'We were the generation that broke out,' Nancy said. 'I think

I was the first member of my family who went to work, except for a maiden aunt.'

'And you were the eldest?'

'No, second-eldest.'

'Out of how many?'

'Six — there were six. I had five sisters.'

'So where was your father?'

'In Tasmania, he was a minor pastoralist on the Uze River in the Derwent Valley, the next village to Hamilton.'

'How old were you when you married?'

'I was thirty-nine.'

'When did your daughter come along?'

'Helen arrived in 1954, in Hobart.'

'How old were you?'

'Forty-four.'

'What did you think when you found out you were pregnant?'

'I was pleased. She was the only grandchild.'

Lorraine was incredulous. 'The only grandchild from a family of six girls?'

Theodora's Tarn

The Second World War loomed over Theo's early years in Tasmania. Looking through newspapers in the Tasmanian archives, this period was a black hole for mountaineering, with feature stories petering out in 1939 and swinging into print again in 1945. We asked Nancy if there was much in the newspapers about the Walking Club during the war.

'I shouldn't think so,' she said.

'Why was that? Was it inappropriate?'

'I was secretary during the war and we had thirty-seven members,' she said. And after all, who wanted to read about a few people clambering over a mountain, when we were engaged in a world war?'

'Were there many women in the Walking Club?'

'Fifty-fifty.'

Of course if the Japanese, or Germans for that matter, had landed and got a toehold in the Tasmanian wilderness, it would have been a different matter if Theo and her friends were commandeered to lead the resistance. However, the members of the Launceston Walking Club were not thus tested.

Nancy's daughter, Helen Moore, commented that they were an amazing group, walking as they did with other women's husbands and fiancés. I couldn't resist asking if there were any romances on the mountains.

Nancy's reply was short and sharp: 'Other people had romances — we didn't.'

'There are numerous photos of men and women, including Theo's and Smithies', resting on those impossibly thin plinths of rock known as tarns. Are they difficult to climb?'

'There's generally some way round them,' she said.

On the subject of tarns, there were three Frederick Smithies photos, in Theo's collection, of a lakeside camping site called Theodora's Tarn. While there's hardly a tall rock formation in sight, Theodora appears to be perched on a small boulder rising from the water. Is Theodora's Tarn a real place name, or is it a private location known to a select few? Indeed, Nancy claimed not to know where it was.

To climb a mountain is a lifetime goal for a select few. Theo's account of climbing Frenchman's Peak in Tasmania invites the reader to share in the joyful preparation, anticipation and camaraderie leading up to the attempt by the three adventurous young women.

May 1944

On Good Friday, having risen at half-past six, I had five cups of tea and some cheese on toast, wearing my blue dressing gown until I was almost ready to leave the house. I put on ironed walking pants in a manner pertaining to the civilised world, smoothed a blouse collar over my sweater, so that both were attractively exposed beneath a green jerkin adorned with a large woollen flower, followed by scarlet socks and boots. There was an anticipatory pleasure in pulling on mountain boots in the heart of civilization. And then, heaving my rucksack over my shoulders, I left to catch a Service Car in preference to a taxi, because taxis have an unpleasant habit of not appearing until the last minute, leaving me with nervous exhaustion.

Frenchman's Cap was my destination and as Cliffy was going to Lake St Clair, we joined forces at the bus. I looked so jaunty in my hiking outfit that she hardly recognised me, expecting no doubt that I went tramping in the hills looking like a down-at-heel degenerate. Contrary to my advice on what to wear for Lake St Clair, she appeared in a dashing black outfit, her saving grace being that she wore sensible shoes.

We reached the highest point of Tasmania, where heath-covered moors and open country is dotted with small rocky hills close by the Great Lakes. Seeing the large expanse of the Great Lake for the first time, stretching away like an inland sea, is something you never forget. Afterwards when Cliffy was so captivated by the beauty of Lake St Clair and could talk of nothing else, I asked her if she had forgotten the stunning sight of the Great Lake, because to me, while Lake St Clair has a unique beauty, it cannot compare with the magnificence of the Great Lake.

We had morning tea at the Rainbow Chalet, a facility that more of Tasmania's remote beauty spots would benefit from. A further twenty miles on, the bus had pretty well followed the lakes edge until we'd turned and veered across the plains. Reaching the Missing Link section of the road we plunged down, down, down, through gum forests to the bare plain country of Bronte, and the junction of the Launceston and Hobart roads, to the West Coast. We were at the stage of the journey where we needed to stretch and get rid of the kinks. Extending a leg, I inadvertently drove a mountain-booted foot into the ankle of the person in front. My quick apology was met with stunned, pained silence.

...

On the way to Derwent Bridge there was a wonderful view of the blue wedge-shape of imposing Mount Olympus, and further on the magical sickle-shape of Mount Rufus where we passed a party of boys with rucksacks, travelling in an old breakdown T-model Ford.

We arrived at the Derwent Bridge Hotel where I was meeting my walking companions, Steve and Nance, but there was no sign of them yet. As the hotel had a dining room full of travellers, we waited on the steps: Cliffy for transport to Lake St Clair and myself for the bus from Hobart, bringing my two friends. Different people I knew from Hobart and the St Clair Hydro Electric plant had joined us for a natter, cluttering up the steps, when the T-model Ford lurched into sight, towed by a car, which turned off towards St Clair. The Ford was then unhitched and, like rabbits out of a hat, six boys, all shapes and sizes, came tumbling out. One wore white boots while another looking like a direct descendant of Ned Kelly, had on an ancient footy Guernsey emboldened with a prominent number thirteen. Several came up the steps, entering the hotel, and when they returned to their automobile they all pushed and shoved together, until they had it rolling into one of the hotel sheds, whereupon somebody mentioned they'd heard that these fellows were also walking to Frenchman's Cap.

Shortly afterwards the Service Cars from Hobart arrived and I saw Steve straightaway, wearing a flamboyant sombrero and serviceable-looking jodhpurs, followed by Nance, less noticeable, but dressed for some serious bushwalking. Three more men, retiring academic types from Hobart, were also bound for the Cap. We three girls were starving, and heading for the hotel dining room, we luckily secured seats. When Fergie arrived to collect people staying at Lake St Clair, Cliffy poked her head into the room and we all waved goodbye.

An hour later we were packed into a bus, a sympathetic driver allowing us to travel together through a National Park of myrtle forests enclosed by mountains to King William Saddle and on to the aptly named Surprise Valley. Here we saw a dramatic transition, accomplished within only a few feet, from the cropped grass of the moor uplands on the King

William Mountains to a luxuriant profusion of myrtles, sassafras and manferns in a valley enclosed by mountainous walls. And in the midst of the forested valley a sharp, conical wooded hill stood. The road wended down, down, requiring great driving skill, until some nine miles further on a signpost announced 'Frenchman's Cap'.

On leaving the Service Car we observed the Dunsinane-like movements of a bush, which turned out to be one of the three men from Hobart, discarding a sweater or two. Of the six boys there was no sign. And we guessed that they were probably four miles up the track, galloping along with that wild recklessness that young males usually exhibit on the mountain.

...

Steve, Nance and I set out along the track. I'd imagined having to fight our way through horizontal fagus and giant button-grass, and I was more than glad to find the path free of obstacles and as clear and untroubled as our hearts. With the Franklin River only a few minutes from the trail, we could hear the boisterous gargling of the stream bouncing along a bed of pebbles. The track wound upwards a little, before it passed over undulating country with gums and earth razed black by a bushfire. And then just over the rise, we were drawing great gulps of ice-edged wilderness air and expelling our city business cares, when there was a commotion at our heels. Number 13 was leading when the six boys passed us at breakneck speed like a string of camels.

'Arrgg!' we all cried. And then Nance said, 'There they go, we won't see them again unless it's on top of the mountain.'

Through the burnt gums the track went and we removed a sweater or so, proceeding under and over fallen trees through slightly undulating country, until the track decided it was time to stop playing about and get down to business and aimed for the sky. Well, we nearly fell over them, with our heads bent, plodding steadily up — all six of them, lying about on the sides of the track: those same six boys, and for some unknown reason one of them was wearing a cape-groundsheet. This passing and re-passing continued until we reached our camping spot. While we tramped at a steady and ceaseless pace, the boys zoomed ahead and then stopped to catch their breath, lost somebody, waited for somebody else and zoomed ahead again, and again, and again! It may have been companionable for us out there in the wilderness, but it wasn't exactly restful.

...

Having reached the ridge, the track stopped dishing out 'a taste of things to come' and the next stage can only be described as 'bewitching', with the path pottering happily over bare honey-golden hills with glimpses of the King William Mountains on the left. We came to the end of the Franklin hills and before us lay the enticing panorama one sees from so many places, from Mount Rufus, Mount Gould, all the Reserve Mountains, the Barron Hills gashed with the opening of the Pass and beyond, and the splendid white head of the Frenchman's Cap. To rush ahead with hardly a glance at such a scene would be sacrilege and we stayed a while, seated on our packs, committing the outline to memory.

Next it became the chameleon track plunging down bare grassy hills; golden-yellow hills; a white track following a little stream dancing along its own quartzite bed until we were running down to where the hills levelled out on a button-grass plain. We tramped along, discussing the vagaries of musicians in wartime Tasmania. I happened to be leading and from time to time half-turned my head so the others could hear what I was saying. To emphasise one point I turned right around — and behold! Those six boys were plodding along behind Nance and Steve, not uttering a word, so that we three had been unaware of their presence.

We strung out across the beautiful desolate plain like a caravan of African porters on safari. The track soon crosses this wide valley, which is confined by little wooded hills, to reach a grove of dead timber and many bridges over the unattractive Lodden River — or should we say, unattractive bridges over the unattractive Lodden. The water of this stream is the colour of strong tea, the current is swift, but it is silent. The water seems heavy, so that where it runs over stones or against fallen gums it has no joyous note: there is no sound.

We three girls found the many bridges trying to our patience and nerves. Steve saved my morale by saying in her vigorous voice, 'It's just the idea of not having anything to hold onto that upsets us. If we had only a piece of cotton beside us we wouldn't mind at all.' 'Well!' said Steve, with her customary conviction and energy, 'Let's imagine that piece of cotton!' Personally I did, but the idea fell flat when we came to a very high bridge — this is a courtesy title as these 'bridges' are merely great fallen trees. It was too daunting and we took to an alternative tree at the water's edge. Steve went first and got her feet wet, and Nance was next and got the seat of her pants wet. I followed last and benefitted by their experience, arriving on the other side of the stream quite dry, feet and seat.

The track became indistinct and difficult to follow through this patch, and when it arrived at an open button-grass plain we stopped right in the middle for a two or three minute rest. It is delightfully easy to sit down with a heavy pack on a tussock, but it is remarkably awkward to get up again. Nance wanted a strap tightened and Steve obliged, but between the insecure footing and having a fit of the giggles, Nance ended up face first in a tussock. When we were finally all upright again, a few moments later, we were obliged to search for the track which had become overgrown with a thick belt of scrub. Once on track we were regaled with some remarkable loud and sweet bird song. The Tasmanian bush is ordinarily very silent and devoid of birdsong and I found the sudden cheerfulness of the birds disturbing. We moved across another button-grass patch, with the blue Barron Hills on our right, and at our feet purple-lipped flowers grew in the track.

Soon we came to another wooded patch, and near the last bridge of the Lodden we noticed where there had been a camp, with tent-poles remaining as a fixture. The time was right, the place definitely right, and we made our first camp. We had only been walking for three hours, but it was close to nightfall.

. . .

The night was warm and mild, and after we had our tea we turned in, just at dusk. I slept in between the two girls and subsequent events seemed to indicate that it was in the wrong place. What a night! I kept waking up to find myself well out of my rightful position: once with my head in the long-suffering Nance's stomach; once with Steve breathing heavily down my ear; once with my head near the tent-fly, right up against Nance's feet, my own feet perilously close to Steve's face, so that finally I kept waking up and lying pathetically for a moment, trying to get my bearings. The mosquitoes kept up a ceaseless noise, dive-bombing every now and then to strategic points; the sandflies were very quiet, but they followed the tradition of the Navy.

We rose early, the girls having suffered silently all night, never knowing which sudden threshing movement of mine would maim them forever; and I of course was quite worn out with never knowing quite where I was whenever I woke up. Nance lit the fire while Steve and I had a swim in the Lodden; then it was Nance's turn to wash while we thawed out near the fire.

'Ah, the joys of camping!' I cried, ecstatically, trying to inhale snatches of fresh air through the smoke of the fire.

An hour later we broke camp, unaffected by the intermittent light rain. Our objective, the mountain, was hidden by Barron Pass, and the Pass was immersed in cloud. We walked steadily over the button-grass plain until we reached a sign post with the sign 'Frenchman's Cap' attached to the base of the post. We were on the Jane River Track and the sign indicated a branch-off called Philip's Lead, which we became convinced that everybody we knew who'd come this way had missed, because they never talked about how beautiful it was.

We had discovered the real beginning, with a line of stakes indicating the way to go, plunging across the button-grass tussocks in a ragged line. It was the most beautiful valley, with a broad golden stream, cascades of green timbered hills on the right, and strange white mountainous walls on the left. On and on we walked, our packs thumping against our livers, when at times we jumped from tussock to tussock. For this trip we were obliged to carry our tent and we took it in turns. There was many a good-natured argument as to whose turn it was to carry it and how we hated the moment when it was our turn to carry the additional weight, although nobody actually said so.

. . .

I'd packed a billy, heavy with soaking materials for a stew, and I virtuously announced my intentions to make 'a rich, classical stew that will take us to the top of the mountain in a leap and a bound', when it was almost my turn with the tent. 'Imagine how good you will feel standing beside the fire, wrapping yourself around a chop and bacon stew, thick with lentils...'

'Stop!' cried Nance and Steve together, insisting — still in unison — on taking a turn to carry the stew. That damned stew! It became a ritual when the tent changed from one person, the stew would likewise change hands.

Our track took us up a steep hillside timbered with myrtle, past dead and decaying myrtles, artfully ornamented with moss and delicate pink epacris bells. The damp air was sweet with sassafras. In the myrtle forests, where the light itself seemed to be green, we came upon little scarlet toadstools and knotted mossy roots between the earth-mould of decaying leaves, harboured bright orange fungi. The tranquil beauty soothed our senses and the imagination readily conjured a dun-faced gnome, his hands gnarled like the roots, his jerkin as green as the trees, his pointed hat the scarlet of the toadstools and his snapping black eyes those of the unafraid mountain thrushes. We plodded on up the steep path in that pleasant ease of companionship, whereupon each engages her own thoughts and silence is unbroken. The path finally emerged on top of the myrtle-clad hill, crossed some swampy button-grass, ambling along a button-grass valley beside little moulded hills, until a concave valley dotted with gums was reached at the foot of which Lake Vera lies.

We were pleasantly surprised to find that the group of boys had seen us coming down the gum rise and had made morning tea for everyone in the most enormous billy we had ever seen. Heavy clouds hanging over the Pass drifted across the black water of the lake, and it rained lightly as we sat on our packs and heard how the boys had eaten unbelievable quantities of sausages, and quaffed unprecedented numbers of mugs of tea, when they reached their camping spot after dark the previous night.

Once again Nance and I feared that we would have to grapple heroically with dreadful logs, horizontal and richea in unnerving quantities. It was a pleasant surprise when traversing the lakeside to find that except for some slightly boggy patches and a few fallen trees it was an excellent track. It wound around the end of the lake until we reached the myrtle forest where we stopped for lunch, making our fire from fragrant chips of Huon pine. At the very edge of the lake feathery reeds with tassels rustled and swayed in the breeze. A huge, fallen myrtle lay caught in the top of the forked limbs of a living tree, its base supported by another fallen-giant. Its whole length was covered with many kinds of mosses as well as a veritable garden of epacris. At the very edge of the lake, feathery reeds with tassels rustled and swayed in the breeze.

After lunch, we proceeded up the track, and at one stage it would have been easier using a stepladder, since hauling oneself up a steep slope by an inch or so of root, plus the encumbrance of a billy of stew, is a poor way to spend your leisure. At another stage when I was leading, the scrub seemed impenetrable to the left and the steep creek banks were immediately on the right. The track plunged into a fallen tree and so did I. I only extricated myself by lying on my back, rolling on my side and wriggling various limbs and trunk like an eel with convulsions. My furious threshing, following the track out of the tree, prevented me from hearing if the others were following. And when at last the pack and body finally ejected themselves out of the tree, I saw the two girls madly struggling with it in their turn and noticed an apologetic little subsidiary track, starting in the middle of a richea bush and plunging over a precarious cascade of rocks to the right of the obstruction.

We climbed higher and higher, until we reached a dry creek-bed of mossy stones where we followed an axe-blazed trail on the tree trunks.

When the clouds cleared we found ourselves surrounded by a solid semi-circle of mountain walls. A fall of stones that looked like a track, swung away, disappearing under one of the walls and we seemed trapped in a basin of rock. But then, with a wall of rock on our right, the snow-gums to the left lured us straight ahead like white posts keeping traffic on the highway. We climbed up and over a stone-fall beneath the cliff and from there it was simply a case of following the blazed track to the top of the Pass.

'I'd forgotten how rugged this section was,' Steve panted, stopping short of complaining about carrying my stew, 'or I wouldn't have packed those extra snacks.'

We arrived at the top breathless and sat on the rocks gazing at the beetling prow of Frenchman's Cap. It felt like sitting on the edge of the world. The proud bulwark rose with waves of hills at its feet and clouds racing across its mighty white quartzite face, engulfing it and then retreating, carrying the threat of rain. Far below lay two lakes in a broad forested valley, while a third peeped from a hill to the right, under the mountain. The width of the Barron Pass is only a few feet, with precipices to the right and left. We ate some chocolate and I smoked a pensive cigarette, while Nance worried about the timing needed to photograph the magnificent scenery.

A few precious minutes rest and we were on the move again, swinging on our packs and plunging down through the trees and then up to where a notice commanded us to, 'Keep Up'. Debating whether this was meant to be a moral booster or advice for the track, we decided it was the latter when the track continually petered out, only to pop up again with not too much searching. Under the huge peaks we went, over heath and great rock falls until we came to our campsite for the night.

The Thumbs, two wooded peaks, stood at one end, looking like a medieval castle and a little richea ridge seemed to keep the narrow valley of silvery pineapple grass from tumbling down to the hills far below. Nance and I were romanticising, saying that it was an enchanted place, when Steve reminded us that it was time to pitch camp, and she muttered darkly to me, 'That stew of yours had better be good.'

We made a huge fire for the stew, put up the tent and cut pandani leaves for sleeping on. But the stew refused to cook and how unpleasant a quarter-burned, uncooked lentil-rice-carrot-chop-bacon mess can taste! Accursed stew! We'd cursed it while scaling the Barron Pass, we cursed it as we tried to eat it and we cursed the after-effects. No stew can, in some circumstances, be a good stew!

Our substitute meal was cold chicken supplied by Nance, and Steve's biscuits. We drank coffee and watched the moon rise from behind the odd-shaped battlements of the hills and the Pass. The pale disk, gliding into a sky still rosy from the last rays of the sun, cast an ethereal light over the rippling lines of hills far below. Soon the stars shone brilliantly and the Southern Cross hung above.

...

We were up early the next morning. From our perch we saw mist swathing the hills below: a gossamer wrap retreating ahead of the sun. It looked like a good day for our climb and we were elated. We left at quarter past eight and arrived at Lake Tahune an hour later. It is small and deep, surrounded by hills except at its outlet. From one end rises the white Frenchman's Cap, as uncompromising a mass as I ever saw. This must rise, almost sheer, about two thousand feet from the lake's edge, in layers of colour — the silver-green of pineapple grass, the green of rather stunted myrtles and great pandanis, the brown of a thick layer of earth and rock and then the white quartzite of the Cap.

We left our packs and set off with sweaters and windproof jackets tied around our waist. Steve was humming out of sheer joy, Nance had a gleam in her eye, but I felt slightly like Dopey trailing along in the rear. I thought of all the things I'd rather do than climb that intimidating rock. The Col is almost 1000 feet of steep earth, with wet millegania where creeks have been, over rock-falls, and finally over the lip of the Col where snow lay. We kicked steps up to the top, and crouched for a moment to survey the world from our unique vantage point. Lake Tahune looked like a tiny mirror shard ringed with high grassy hills, down which plunged a creek. Halfway down the creek little trees grew as its attendants. The trees became larger and larger towards the lake's edge, giving the appearance of a cascade. On the edge of the lake grew a rich profusion of pandani, pencil pines, pineapple grass and some myrtle.

We had climbed up a green way of millegania, richea and berry bushes. But, looking down the other side of the Col, lay a world as desolate and barren as the moon craters. The white ramparts of the Cap sank down to a valley higher than the level of Tahune, and within it lay another lake, bleak and desolate. White rocks, white walls and white boulders enclosed this unhappy lake, with no speck of green anywhere to be seen. We took one last look at the Tahune valley, and I wondered if the Cap is ever reflected in the Lake, and could imagine no more breathtaking or more beautiful a jewel. We walked towards the Cap.

'Climb that chimney?' Nance said. 'Never!'

And I thoroughly agreed.

Steve said thoughtfully, 'It's possible.'

We searched a little further, considering one or two possible but unpleasant alternatives to reach the summit, and then tramped around the cliffs to have a look there — but up they soared for a thousand feet: great walls gashed with savage chasms. We clung to the cliff face, sheltering from the strong, keen wind, and wondered what to do next: three tiny midges in a world of stone!

After a little while we decided to have another look at the first chimney. Had we but known, the correct track lay slightly below the level of the Col and the Lake Tahune side, but there we were, near our chimney.

Suddenly, Steve said, 'Gosh! We can get up there!'

The wind made me lose my nerve for a minute.

'But look — there and there and there.'

Nance and I looked, and sorrowfully reminded each other that doubtless there were hardy spirits who would have spurned this as being too easy — but not we two. However Steve was soon up; Nance went next and then me. It was an unpleasant and unfriendly chimney; once on top it seemed that I was doomed to stay on the mountain forever, for it is as a rule far harder getting down. However, we had won our mountain, because the way up to the cairn was steep, but very easy. There was another chimney near the top, but an easy, very knobbly one. Then we were on the broad brow of the cap, on a gentle pebbly rise, little stakes marching through the snow to the cairn.

This gentle slope seemed to be a fit crown for the giant: a crown on which grew and blossomed sturdy everlastings. We had a sense of the peace of the hills; this noble head seemed the epitome of beauty, a fit ending to the mighty barricade of cliffs and savage ridges below. From the cairn we gazed at the knife-edge of cliffs and wild ridges below; we looked over at Barron Pass, on which we had stood but yesterday; we gazed at the lakes, the wooded valleys, the hills falling wave on wave to the horizon. Peaks of almost the height of the Cap lay crowned or wreathed with mist — and thus we sat on the cairn storing up the memory for other days when we would be back with the other poor mortals in the cities in the paralytic grip of civilization.

The wind was icy, and we soon had very cold hands. At a much slower pace, three women satiated with beauty sauntered back down the heath and rock indented track; down the fateful chimney — somehow; down over the snow of the Col-lip and down to Tahune. Fortune continued to smile on us as the boys, seeing three tiny figures moving along the skyline, prepared steaming mugs of cocoa for us, and we had no sooner arrived at the Tahune camp than rain pelted down, and the Hobart men arrived at the same moment.

...

We ate our lunch, and then set off in the steady rain for our camp under the Thumbs. Alas for our socks drying on the bushes! How damp it was! We packed up wetly, shouldered the wet tent, wet packs, and set off for the Lake Vera camp. The misty rain made the towering cliffs seem incredibly high, imposing and awful coming down the Pass. It took us three hours to reach the damp forest and make camp. It was a miserable place with the rain darkening the already green light of the myrtles. After a brief evening meal we got out of our wet clothes into our only dry things — sleeping bags and pyjamas. With our heads dripping wet and our feet in the rain we huddled miserably together in the wet little tent.

Next morning I awoke to find that my knees were swollen to the size of two footballs. Fluid on the knees, out in the wilderness, was a potentially serious predicament. However, I still had some motive power left and was able to move my legs like a couple of rusty pistons with a little coercion. The rain did not let up, but we had to be on our way. Removing our pyjamas, we wrapped them in the sleeping bags to keep them dry for the night and emerged nude into the inhospitable morning. When it came to dressing, we wrung out our socks, singlets, trousers and sweaters, emptied the water from our boots and donned wet windproofs and headgear. Too unhappy to light a fire, we packed up, becoming more drenched with each passing moment.

Theo's Frenchmen's kneecaps

Frederick Smithies gave Theo a magnificent photo of his ascent of Frenchmen's Cap. He wrote on the back: 'Lake Tahune where we camped right at the foot of Cap for six nights. Notice two tents near left corner of lake, away down nearly 1000 feet below. We were climbing up to ridge at base of final summit of the Cap which was almost a 1000 feet above us still.' Friend and writing mentor Smithies wanted Theo to use his photos in the book she was writing, which was about the Tasmanian wilderness. But first she had to recover from her Frenchmen's Cap injury:

The sun burst through the clouds when we were on the gum ridge on the other side of Lake Vera and the rain nearly stopped, giving us the incentive to stop and make a really delicious breakfast of eggs, bacon and coffee. The clearing in the weather, however, was temporary and after half-an-hour on the homeward track we were again deluged. We spent the day tramping steadily, for with my knees we knew we must get as close to the road as possible, since we were catching the Queenstown Service Car at 10am the next day.

The rivers of our track were flooded and it was a challenge negotiating the really high bridge that we had previously avoided wearing a pack. At 4pm we reached our camping spot within ten minutes' walk of the road and now in considerable pain I lay in my sleeping bag, cushioned by a bed of bracken in the tent and everybody waited on me with tea and food. Steve erected a peculiar structure of saplings near the fire and the foliage became a makeshift clotheshorse of gloves, socks, sweaters and panties: muddy all of them and smelly to an incredible degree. In the morning we prised mud from our boots, fossicked for lipsticks and tried to look like three intrepid mountaineers. It was back to civilization and a fortnight in bed for me with Frenchman's kneecaps.

Chapter 14
Theo
History required the invisibility of women

Theo's 1940s writing was devoid of any social analysis or feminist awareness. Typical of a young woman raised and educated with patriarchal values, she'd pulled the shades over her mother's collective past. 'Until the 1970s,' wrote Marilyn Lake in *Getting Equal: The History of Australian Feminism*, 'the writing of Australian history was marked by the absence of women. This was no accident, nor was it an easily corrected oversight. For, as the public record of men's deeds, history rested on — in fact required — the invisibility of women. History was the self-conscious record of the white men who made the nation.'[1]

Man with a Marble Brain

Living in a world controlled by men and filled with male sculptures, Theo demonstrated that she had inherited her mother's propensity to pen character sketches. Her poem 'Man with a Marble Brain', about a male sculpture on a Launceston building, was sent to Ethel on 2 November 1942:

Sculptured you sit and watch the passing crowds;
Strange to look there and see larger than life
Your seated figure with its downcast face;
Hands relaxed and arms between your knees.
Idly the flag, half lowered in the evening wind,
Caresses both your shoulders and your head.
The slender arc of moon above dreams too,

If dreams stir in your marble brain. Strange
That your maker caught your pensive melancholy,
And you so unresponsive. You seem so real.
Gold slender moon and you seem eternal things.
Sadness and beauty; and softly, blindly,
The flag flutters unreasoning in the chilly breeze.

Tasmania engulfed by return servicemen

At the end of World War II, the job security of the women who'd kept the country running during the exodus of the fighting men was in jeopardy. Could this be the flag fluttering 'unreasoning in the chilly breeze' in 'Man with a Marble Brain'? Does Theo's writing about men in Launceston streets betray anxiety? Is she searching for a way of 'breaking free of the unconscious boundaries created by cultural expectations'?[2] What are the society and family expectations for an almost thirty-year-old woman?

1 July 1945

As I am leaving Launceston soon, I want to remember a few things. There is a very straight, shabby old man with whiskers whom I sometimes see in the streets. The whiskers are stained with either nicotine or tannin, but they still manage to be patriarchal, and not to look repellent. And his eyes are most attractive: they smile at one with childish candour and it isn't trite to say they smile with sweetness. Although he has the face of an old man, he must be an old man with the right sort of philosophy, for his face is kindly in expression. If he is shabby and old, he is also straight and dignified; his thoughts must have led him to be happy in this world, but not how to get this world's goods. He stands and watches the passing crowds sometimes and I gaze straight into his smiling blue eyes.

Another person I've noticed about the town is a dapper, clean-shaven, slightly portly man, who has a box arrangement on the back of his motor-cycle in which he carries flowers. When this man sits on his motor-cycle, and you are directly behind him, as he is practically invisible, it is a special thrill to watch when he turns around corners. His seat is very erect and dignified, the quality of dignity being enhanced by a bowler hat. There is also another man, and while I cannot remember details, the front basket of his bicycle and general floral effect are unforgettable.

Of course there are other purveyors of goods, and one day I witnessed a small boy upsetting his basket of sausages onto the road. Needless to say he simply raised the strings of them back from the mire and packed them back into the basket. One only sees this sort of thing once in a lifetime and it is well to record it.

Horse-cabs Only

Why was Theo drawn to write about men in Launceston streets rather than women? Had she, like her mother before her, realised that only material written on the subject of men, or material written by men, was taken seriously?

There is also a very dejected man with a very dejected, unhappy-looking horse and a most dejected, unhappy dog. The dilapidated vegetable cart which all three attend looks as if it will one day, like the old soldier, simply fade away. They are altogether an incredible group and we pass each other every day.

Under a sign 'Horse-cabs Only' may be seen all day and every day, Launceston's only Horse-cab. The horses are in good condition, one being white and the other black. These animals stand so long in the one position that they get rather bored with life, and their feet assume the oddest positions. Sometimes they seem to be talking to each other as horses will, and I have seen some delightful expressions on the face of the white one. The black horse must know a few risqué stories.

At the pinnacle of her career

Theo was at the pinnacle of her career, a successful businesswoman, who had pioneered sport and recreation for women, and her future looked promising indeed. She had left a significant footprint on the island state. What happened next is puzzling indeed!

Everyone has been very nice to me for the last few weeks and I suppose I've been smiling more than was actually necessary. As a farewell gift I went on a Board inspection trip up Mount Barrow. There wasn't any snow on the mountain — in fact there wasn't any water, because everything was frozen stiff with ice cascades, pools of ice, ice on the rocks and ice in sheets. This was my third trip up Barrow and the only successful one. On the first, with the Branagans, we had car trouble at the first hut and were only able to gaze at the cliffs above and on the second with the Horsfalls, I decided to get out of the car near the top and walk up via one of the chimneys. A foolish decision, for one shouldn't walk alone. I got into difficulties on wet, steep rocks and had to retrace my steps, reaching the carpark just as the cars were ready to return to Launceston.

But on this last trip we went right up to the car-turning place and then started peregrinations. We walked up to the end of the skyline track, and it is most dramatic, being right on the edge of the cliffs. There was a swirling mist boiling up through the chimneys, and it was wonderful to stand at the edge of the void, among the icy crags, to gaze into — well, nothing except a movement of mist and wind between jagged outlines of rock. When the path ended, we scrambled among rocks for some distance, until an enormous hunger drove us back to lunch at the car park hut. After that effort we walked around as much mountain as possible between then and darkness. A most wonderful sunset flamed below us, making the world seem remote and its cares and responsibilities petty and unimportant.

...

After my swansong and farewell to Tasmania, I had an unexpected return. There followed a series of wonderful weekends up Ben Lomond. The war was over and members of the Club were returning from the Services. Consequently, one was invited to make up a party, instead of, as during the past few years, struggling to go up the mountain.

Theodora Fitzpatrick should certainly be counted in Naomi Wolf's estimation of the untold numbers of young women who give the impression that the rights they enjoy were granted to them by a naturally evolving society that grew ever more enlightened about women without any pressure from them. Indeed, the implications of the feisty Fitzpatrick's ignorance of where women really stood in the scheme of things in conservative 1940s Tasmania, as she sought to publish a book about women conquering a hereto male domain, are obvious to us in hindsight. Naomi Wolf describes the visible adversaries that kept generations of Australian women, including Theo, in the dark about women's snail's pace progress to equality:

> If it were history books alone that deleted the women's movement, women could still turn to contemporary media to document their changing status. But the mainstream media leave out women in general, and the women's movement in particular, with a comprehensiveness that has disturbing implications for democracy.[3]

Theo had her seventy-eighth birthday in 1993, the year that Wolf published *Fire with Fire*. Marilyn Lake's *Getting Equal: The History of Australian Feminism*, was published in 1999, the year after Theo died at the age of eighty-two, and four years before the death of Theo's contemporary, artist Nora Heysen, who was the first woman to break the previously all-male mould when she won the Archibald Prize for portraiture in 1938.[4]

Who is your most admired person in history?

On Friday 25 November 2011, the annual lecture of the History Council of Australia at the State Library of Victoria, presented by Dr Clare Wright, was promisingly titled *Mothers of the Revolution: Sex, Suffrage and the Birth of a Nation*. I wasn't disappointed, as Wright drew on her research for her ABC TV documentary *Utopia Girls*, with plenty of detail on the life of Vida Goldstein as she elaborated on how women's history is all too easily forgotten.

The following week I had an appointment with a hairdresser, who happened to be an Englishman. We'd never met before and knew nothing about each other, when out of the blue he asked, 'Who is your most admired person in history?' Well! How do you know what you think until you hear what you say?

'Vida Goldstein,' I shot back without hesitation. 'She was invited into the Oval Office in 1902 to meet President Theodore Roosevelt, some fourteen years before an Australian Prime Minister was granted the privilege.'

And then I experienced my own giant step for womankind — it really felt like walking on the moon when the hairdresser was oh-so impressed with my Australian women's suffrage heroine! From a generation of teenage girls denied their basic history and heroines, growing up in a time when the extraordinary accomplishments of women were brushed into the dustbin of humanity, I finally understood the importance of recording the experiences of Mary Ann, Ethel and Theo.

Photographers, writers and artists

Theo Fitzpatrick's excursions into the remote Tasmanian wilderness and her subsequent friendship with photographer Frederick Smithies and his family significantly produced a merging of 'text' and 'image', showcasing the wild paradise, the jewel in the crown, yet to be discovered by Tasmania's largely coastal dwelling population. The pair documented early tourism and recreation in the island state. They were both involved with accessing the wilderness and the bushwalking clubs to which they belonged, and respected the bounteous beauty at their doorstep. Not so the politicians and custodians of Tasmania's unique heritage, with a shameful record of seventy-five years of dam building and destruction in the name of progress.

Was Theo Fitzpatrick a unique example of young Australian women of the 1940s, or did she simply embody the spirit of the times? Just four years older than Theo, artist Nora Heysen saw Damian Parer's New Guinea photographs of 'Fuzzy Wuzzy Angels' supporting soldiers, and offered her skills as an official war artist.[5] This should have been a breeze for the Archibald Prize winner, but in 1943, after she enlisted as Captain Heysen and walked the Kokoda Trail, she risked court martialling for the subjects she painted and was irked by the limitations placed on her.[6] In an interview with Janet Hawley, Heysen explained her position:

> They didn't want a woman, didn't know what to do with me, what I should wear, which sector I should belong to. I wanted to get as close as I could to the action, and finally was sent to New Guinea under the military history department, with the direction to paint women in uniform. But there wasn't anything of women to see! In that hot climate they were covered head-to-heel in khaki uniforms, long trousers, leggings, long sleeves, netting over their hats. And khaki is a dreadful colour to paint. The men in jungle greens made far more appealing subjects.[7]

Frederick Smithies was a different photographer to that other denizen photographer of the wilderness, Peter Dombrovskis, in that he was a portrayer of heroic figures in the landscape. Smithies' figures are statuesque, as they stand or sit on high vantage points. They are dominant in a conquered landscape, in grand-scale mountain photos such as: *Mount Barrow*; *On the Acropolis, Du Cane Range*; *Theo near the Pinnacle of Cradle Mountain, with Lake Rodway below*; *Young woman sketching Cradle Mountains with Lake Wilkes and Lake Dove below*; *Summer Trip, Ben Lomond*; and *Theodora on Whymper Crags, Ben Lomond, October 1947*.

Frederick Smithies and the 'Ben'

Frederick Smithies' first ascent of Frenchman's Cap was from Queenstown, in March 1931:

> Smithies was the founder of the Northern Tasmanian Alpine Club, which was largely responsible for the opening-up of Ben Lomond as skiing country. He also founded the Launceston Walking Club on 29 November 1946, and was its patron from the start. The automobile has robbed Tasmania of much of its isolation, and led to the ruination of much of its best-loved areas and extreme scarcity of native fauna. But in members of these clubs an awareness of our beautiful surroundings was keenly aroused, and areas otherwise quite isolated became accessible, as people like Smithies re-opened old tracks or blazed new ones.[9]

Smithies wrote in 1935:

> Tasmania, for its size, is one of the most rugged and mountainous places in the world. There are, of course, many mountains adjacent to the cities which afford splendid opportunities for more or less strenuous scrambles, according to the desire of the climbers. During the winter months and right through to the end of spring the 'Ben' is the centre of activities of the Northern Tasmanian Alpine Club for Winter Sports. A comfortable chalet has been erected at the 4000 feet level, and here for practically six months in the year parties of members and visitors gather almost every weekend. For the first time in history, a State Ski Championship meeting was held at Legge's Tor in August of this year.[8]

Living and working in Hobart and Launceston, Theo was a member of the Northern Tasmanian Alpine Club and the Launceston Walking Club. She was among the first women to enter what was until then the men's domain of hiking and skiing. She forged lifelong friendships, chasing the bright bubble of the wilderness and capturing it forever with her compulsive writing. In 1946, Theo finished writing a book about Tasmania, and Smithies, her long-time climbing associate, gave her a collection of Tasmanian wilderness photos to illustrate her unique account.

The heavy cameras Smithies carried in the wilderness were an added burden in difficult terrain.[10] He had a magnificent collection of photos that he had taken and processed himself. In 1975, an archivist from the Tasmanian Archives Office examined, selected and copied some 800 photos.[11] In 2005, when Lorraine Secen and I looked at the Frederick Smithies collection, it was our impression that the archivist had neglected to chronicle the first independent women engaged in bushwalking, mountaineering and skiing in Tasmania from the late 1930s onward, because there were no duplications of the photos given to Theo by Smithies for her book. At the time that Theo was writing to her mother about Smithies receiving royal recognition for his promotion of the wilderness, and while she was finishing her book, the process of shoving her out of sight had already begun:

Perhaps you heard, or rather read, that Smithies was included in the King's Birthday honours, and received the OBE. He said Jean was really thrilled but the kids weren't a bit interested, as they had been to the Grammar School Ball the night before, and were thrilled to bits looking at their own pictures in the paper, and blow Daddy!

28 May 1946

Have finished the book: but don't hold out much hope of getting it published, although Smithies said he loved it. Anyway, you shall have it for Christmas if no-one will publish it. How's that? I may enclose a couple of poems with this. I'm typing some tonight, to send to the *Bulletin, Poetry* and *Meanjin*.

Public visibility of women at work had peaked

The Second World War brought unprecedented opportunities for the employment of women in auxiliaries to the defence forces, industry, transport and human services, and the number of women in the workforce rose fifty percent between 1939 and 1943. These modern young women were more self-centred and their expectations of equality sidestepped the social concerns that were fundamental to the ageing organised feminists:[12]

> In this context of rapid change and with public visibility of women at work never having been higher, their underrepresentation in parliament and public life seemed increasingly anomalous, a denial of women's equality as citizens. Women demanded right of entry into public office, but this no longer conceptualised as offering protection to vulnerable women and girls, at risk in the public domain: a seat in parliament, on a board or commission were now matters of equal rights.[13]

In 1946, Theodora Fitzpatrick finished writing a book about being physically equal to men, climbing mountains, skiing and hiking in Tasmania, and for this she had her hand slapped. This was in the midst of a confrontational climate, hot on the heels of the recognition of Smithies' achievements in the wilderness with an OBE, and with the arrival home of the troops.

Little more than a decade earlier, Australian women were vilified for entering professions in which they competed with men. 'Women workers were represented by male commentators as invaders, usurpers and thieves and as destroyers of men's manhood.'[14] Theo's failure to find a publisher was a tragedy compounded by her ignorance of the iceberg proportions of 1940s adversaries to stories of female adventurers in the Tasmanian wilderness.

6 June 1946

Started work with Kinmont Office Equipment this week and I'm still in Hobart. TAK's offices are quite luxurious, with plum coloured carpets and a wonderful system of lighting. It was quite a wrench leaving CPL when the time came and the last month was an experience I wouldn't willingly repeat: damned hard work and a very confused feeling to be starting a new job. After eight years association with CPL, they were brutally casual with my resignation, although Mr Macdougall and the Launceston branch were genuinely regretful. Considering that I wrote up over £2500 business since January they are losing something. However, it's all over.

15 June 1946

Your little daughter has burst forth this week in the *Bulletin*, or had you noticed? Your questions appear to require answering:

Q. 1: Yes, I have left Chartres. They presented me with a handsome pair of bookends.

Q. 2: Yes, Smithies gave me some photographs for my book, but quite a few of them are my own.

Q. 3: Book neither accepted nor rejected so far. I rang Hazel Osborne to get her to check up for me and she said Mr Morris had read it and was communicating with me. In the face of that she didn't like to ask if it had been accepted. She added further that she doubted if he had actually read it. So we await developments — but not for long: I shall ring next Wednesday.

Q. 4: Zerchos is a mere incidental in my life. I have a three-fold job, Northern Manager of the Kinmont Office Equipment Company, same of Kinmont Business Systems, Consultant division, and principal of Zerchos. (I also write poetry, study, ski and swim — will you give me a job sometime?) So how could I get holidays from Zerchos? They won't be having them anyway in the future. It's a Business College, not a ruddy High School.

24 June 1946

I should be studying Accountancy at the moment, but have a cold and a thick head, so am skipping it, and dropping you a note instead of poring over comparative balance sheets and profit and loss accounts. My job is most interesting — I started, I thought I told you, on the 1st of June. Finishing one job on Saturday and starting another on Monday isn't my idea of the right way of going about things, but TAK was most anxious to have it that way. Did I tell you OBM's sent back the book? They suggested sending it to *Walkabout* to be reproduced serially, but I think, rather than do that, I'll wipe it.

Theo stranded on a midlife plateau

And that was it! Theo Fitzpatrick's book rejection was buried in the middle of a letter to her mother. Her accounts of giant steps for women — the first women's sport and recreation in the pristine, untouched Tasmanian wilderness in the early 1940s, were out of step with post-war sentiment, which was largely aimed at putting women back in their place. Theo glossed over her disappointment with accounts of some marvellous skiing weekends.

30 June 1946

I spent the weekend up the Ben and it was sheer punishment — no mountain has ever treated me so badly, thus far. It rained on us all the way up to the Chalet, which we left at 4.15pm on Saturday and *did* have a grim crossing up to the Summit Hut. On the last plateau before the hut I kept falling over because my body was so cold and I couldn't feel any part of me.

The extreme awfulness was caused by a gale laden with rain and sleet. They had brought a new chum up and with the permission of the leader I was right away in front, but when darkness came down I was at the top of Kicking Horse Pass and the wind was so bad that I thought the others might not attempt it — so I skied back to Little Sticks and waited, wet through, in that wicked wind, for at least a quarter of an hour, before bodies loomed through the mist. Apparently they were coming up so I waited for one of them and then we two pushed on up to the hut.

It snowed all night long — about two feet of wet snow, and continued snowing solidly until quarter-to-two in the afternoon, when we left. It then rained on us all the way to the Chalet, down to the cars. It was a grubby, wet little daughter of yours that arrived home to immediately wash her hair.

Mr Tilley Sr also took severe punishment on the crossing to the Summit Hut. I haven't seen anyone so exhausted or unhappy before. He shook uncontrollably and it was some time before he calmed down. New chums should definitely not be taken above the snow-line in darkness. It's asking for the kind of treatment the mountain turned on us at the weekend. Had a hectic week last week and had better barge off to do some ironing.

Yours, glad to be down at sea-level, Theo.

...

Once again upon the Ben, and what a weekend! We arrived on a cold, still moonlit night, and from the road we could see the top of the mountain enveloped in mist. Walking up through the moonlit forest was an unforgettable experience; and coming up the Big Hill section of the track, we noticed a ring of mist encircling the midnight-blue summit of Ben Nevis. Arriving at the Chalet around 11pm, we disposed of a piece of cake and after buttoning on wind-jackets and caps, fossicking out mitts, ski-boots, skis, etc., we set out for the Summit Hut.

With the snow in an icy condition on the track over the Mount Misery slopes, and also up into the Borrowdale, it was a case of shouldering skis instead of wearing them. We reached the mist upon entering the Borrowdale, but the moonlight diffused through quite sufficiently to illuminate the way. The snow was corrugated, like much magnified ripples on the sea-edge. We tramped over this, guided to our goals by the snow-poles, up over Kicking Horse Pass. Over the first plateau the mist thinned a great deal, and we crossed an eerie white expanse whose horizons were bounded by mist. On the second plateau, we saw the White Tor before us, with a translucent wreath of mist across its summit. And how wonderful the Summit Hut looked, snowed over so that only the outline of the roofs twinkled in the moonlight. Across the plateau a vast moon-bow had encircled the moon.

We awoke rather late on Saturday to the soughing of the wind and that meant bad weather. Sure enough, one glance outside revealed a heavy mist. Being energetic we all buttoned on wind jackets, happily waxed skis and went out into the murk. The mist cleared occasionally during the day, but visibility was practically zero and it commenced snowing at 4pm. A blizzard raged all night and when it hadn't abated by two the following afternoon, the party decided we might as well go home.

The storm centre seemed to have been confined to the top of the mountain, with the mist thinning in the Borrowdale as we descended. And it was a quite clear, though a very dull, afternoon as we ran down the Mount Misery slopes. What a strange band of Antarctic people we looked, and only thirty miles from Launceston! The silence of this part of the mountain was extraordinary after the clamour of the storm above. But it had been snowing a little down here, for all the rocks and the track were freshly covered with a pristine mantle and all the little animals had been using the track. We saw spoors of kangaroos, native cats and badgers, plentifully strewn in our path. The pool of the Chalet was frozen over and the gum trees at the brink were ice-encased, with the leaves bunched together with snow.

Chapter 15

Ethel and Theo

Women's experiences matter

Reading Naomi Wolf's *Fire with Fire*, I became concerned about possible feminist polarisation in the story of the Thwaites-Fitzpatrick women. Had I unconsciously entered the victim/oppressor arena mentioned by Wolf?

> You are either victim or oppressor: you are either for us or against us: you are either a non-sexist woman or a sexist man. Either/or thinking is the natural mental reaction to a perception of scarcity. When people feel they have no options, they cling to the assurances of polarized uncertainties. It is only when people feel rich in confidence and space that they dare to pursue the subtleties of what Gloria Steinem calls both/and thinking. Feminism must embrace this psychology of plenty.[1]

As Wolf said, 'Few will tune into the saga of feminism if they already know how it will end. If we cling to a party line, we bore ourselves and alienate our listeners, who feel that they'll have heard it all before.'[2] How could Ethel's account of the lives of fishermen's families, missing from the history of Queenscliff, and the written experiences of Theo, one of the first women to walk, climb and ski in the Tasmanian wilderness, with the photo evidence missing from the Tasmanian archives, still be relevant today? But then, I read Wolf's core tenets of power feminism and my doubts vanished:

1. Women matter as much as men do.
2. Women have the right to determine their lives.

3. Women's experiences matter.
4. Women have the right to tell the truth about their experiences.
5. Women deserve more of whatever it is they are not getting enough of because they are women: respect, self-respect, education, safety, health, representation, money.[3]

Ethel regrets the humorous omissions

Imagine Ethel and Theo living in a time of social media and the internet! Theo would have self published and plastered Tasmanian wilderness pictures all over Twitter to advertise her book and her Facebook blog. We'd find Ethel in the thick of Twitter, transported far from the fly speck of Mannerim on the Bellarine Peninsula, busy passing on favourites and writing pithy comments about literature, music and philosophy to delight her international followers. Instead, in a different time and place, when Ethel wrote, she didn't expect feedback in her lifetime:

20 July 1948

In looking over my diary, I am sorry I did not record more of the humorous incidents, for there were many. But it appears that I used writing more as the relief of unburdening the mind, perhaps because I thought no one would ever see it. It may be the best thing to destroy it. Yet, because I am to go into hospital for the treatment of a lump in the breast, I decided to leave it and trust to the children's forgiveness if there is anything to hurt or annoy.

I am hoping that they will realise that a Mother is not blind to many things they may think she does not see; but of this I'm sure that no sons could be more thoughtful, helpful and kind than Geoff and Bill, nor any daughter more attentive, kind and loving than Bessie. With Theo so far away, I have been given another daughter's thought and care and I am grateful for it.

Women have the right to determine their lives

The generation whose youthful travel ambitions had been curtailed by WWII, if they were still single and had the fare, now embraced post-war opportunities. Among them were Theo Fitzpatrick and her friend Mona Frawley, who left Australia for a working holiday in Great Britain and Europe, from May 1948 to November 1949. A letter from the chartered accountants Deloitte, Pender Griffiths & Co., sent to Theo care of the Overseas League on 16 February 1949, is headed 'Staff':

> We have now received satisfactory replies from Sir Claude James and from the Overseas League, and we have pleasure therefore in confirming our offer of a position on our audit staff at a commencing salary of £350 per annum, which would be reviewed in October next if your services were satisfactory. We would suggest that you commence on 1st March next and we would be glad to know if this would be convenient to yourself.

However, 'time', which stood still for Theo during the war, did not wait for Ethel. Her daughter's absence was a heartfelt blow when she discovered she had breast cancer, and the unfortunate timing made Theo's 'experience of a lifetime' somewhat bittersweet.

10 August 1948
Dear Mum,

I hope you've been getting the little postcards, which is all I can do to cheer you on your way. Bessie has been super with the news system.

We didn't do anything much last week — I think I gave you the details — because of Mona's foot. On Saturday however, we both got the morning off and went to Callander, having booked into the Creag Dhu Hostel. We had tea and then went for a walk through some beautiful country, through woods, with heather flowering on roadside banks to Loch Katrine, about three miles further up the road.

As we neared Brig o'Turk on the way back to the hostel we were offered a lift by a shooting-car, and although we had only about half a mile to go, we accepted. On taking our turn-off, we came upon a youth who had bagpipes under his arm. We asked him if he could play, and he tucked the animal under his arm, and until he got it going it shrieked like a pig. He sort of biffed it with his elbow and twiddled gadgets on the pipe, scowling like mad and blowing away for dear life. Anyway, after the preliminary gambits, (I nearly choked and could hardly keep a straight face), he played some totally unrecognisable tune. When he stopped blowing the thing whirred gently to a stop — I don't think it was really part of the performance — and we duly praised it up. He told us that his father was teaching him, but his brother was a bonnie piper.

Just then the brother appeared on the road, leading a little black dog, and we all proceeded up to the hostel, where the bonnie piper started up, and the Warden organised reels and dancing. It was grand fun to watch, and they're so energetic. You can even get exhausted watching them. After about one-and-half hours, the piper's cap was passed around and the Warden, who must be a very sociable soul, organised singing from different countries.

During the night the rain just streamed down. But in the morning, although it was dull, it was clear. I was up at seven and one of the boys lent me his paraffin cooker so we were able to get breakfast over and be on the road by 9am. I wanted to climb up Ben Venue, but Mona couldn't on account of her ankle. She walked on back to Callander, and I set off for my hill, walking along Loch Achray the opposite side from the road. A very charming track through banks of heather in flower, and bell heather, and bracken, and woods, until I came to the road and about a quarter of a mile down, left my pack at the Loch Achray Hotel, facing the Trossachs Hotel on the opposite side of the water, and set off.

The track was very good until it got in front of the Ben, and then became just a stream running through the rushes. So I took to my heels and just went up. Not a very good idea to be off the tracks in this country, but there was a lovely view on top, and the flowering hillsides of heather were just wonderful. There wasn't another soul on the mountain and I was very startled when a couple of grouse rose with a whir of wings. The season opens on the 12th and I suppose the heather will do the decent thing and bloom all over Scotland on the same date. At all events, I'll recommend the Trossachs and Ben Venue to anyone, but I still wouldn't swap anything in Tasmania for them. You just wait and see how contented I shall be when I come home.

Edinburgh really is a lovely city — apart from the weather. We came off Arthur's seat by a steep direct route to the Salisbury Crags, and walked along the ridge thereof, sitting on the highest crag at about 8 o'clock. If anything, I liked the view better from the crags. You look directly over the city domes, spires, houses and the castle of Holyroodhouse. Smoke was coming from a lot of chimneys and blowing away gently on the breeze. Sheep were grazing on the crags, and their plaintive bleats sounded just the right note. There were myriads of swallows circling about us too. The weather was dull, but it was clear over the city, although the Firth was rather misty.

We came off the Crags by Holyroodhouse and walked through the public road directly in front. Lila ran off to catch her tram, we escorted Dixie to her bus stop in St Andrews Square and then caught our own tram home, made some Milo, had a little feast and were bathed and in bed by 10.15pm. Twilight is coming earlier these nights — at 9.30 it is really just about dark.

Love to you, and there's an enclosure for Bessie, Theo

And so my paternal grandmother was Scottish

Working and sightseeing around the British Isles in 1948 defined Theodora Fitzpatrick's Australian identity, and sharpened her appreciation of Tasmania. Just as she was forging an affinity with the Scottish people and the Highlands, she came face to face with herself, with the discovery that her paternal grandmother, Christine Westhorpe Fitzpatrick, was Scottish. Years later, when Theo found a portrait of her Scottish grandmother, it became her most treasured memento.

21 August 1948

Dear Mum,

Our time in Edinburgh is nearly at an end, and that hurts a bit: I'm wearing my heart on my sleeve as far as Scotland's concerned. Scotland hasn't nearly as wonderful scenery as I had imagined, but the Scots are delightful. And boy, if I've learned a lesson here it's that love makes literature and art, well literature and poetry anyway. We've greater sheer loveliness in our own land, but they describe the country with superlative adjectives because they love it. When we've had a few centuries to discover that our country has its own beauty and we love it, no matter who has higher mountains or anything else, we'll have a ton of literature and poetry too. That's worth coming over to find out. The Scots mightn't be humorous or very witty, but they are perpetually kind and so friendly and pleasant they literally warm the cockles of your heart.

Bessie's letter dated the 15th arrived today and was joyously welcomed, as letters are from home. And so my paternal grandmother was Scottish! But how Scottish? What was her maiden name and where did she come from? And this Scottish blood that runs in Bessie's veins — where did that come from, and what name please? Although by the time you have this I will be in London again. Do answer these questions.

I felt very grieved about Mother's operation and learning what has actually happened: one can only be thankful though that everything has turned out as it has, with no further dangers. Wouldn't I just be on the other side of the globe at a time like this?

Miss Murray, Mrs M's visitor, has coaxed the wireless into life. How she does it is quite beyond us — we can only get hoots of derision from it: she's been saying very firmly that I've got Scottish blood somewhere in my veins. When Bess's letter came tonight and I told her, she just said, 'Oh, I was quite sure of it!'

Love to you all, Theo.

Theo's indecision — stay or return home?

Snail mail compounded Theodora's isolation, distress and guilt. After an agony of indecision about whether to stay or return home on the first available ocean liner to support her mother and family, Theo stayed and travelled to Europe with Mona Frawlay.

4 September 1948

Dear Mum and Everybody,

First of all I want to ask you, in the altered circumstances at home with Mother's illness, whether you think it would be better for me to try and return home now? I don't want anyone to be noble about this, because I think you know how I feel about this place. It's all a wonderful experience, but home is infinitely better, so if you do think it would be better for me to return, it won't be any hardship on my part. Please consider this and let me know at once, everybody. It certainly is an anxious time for me with Mother ill and the strain on you at home.

Love to everyone, Theo.

Ethel at her lowest ebb

In Geelong Hospital, Ethel was at her lowest when she had her seventy-third birthday, four days after surgery. Theo wrote her a thick wad of letters from Scotland, some running to nineteen pages of tiny script. The dates of these short extracts reveal that they were written after Ethel's first poignant breast cancer diary entry and before her account below:

17 September 1948

Home again, after nearly eight weeks. I went into hospital on 25th July and had surgery for the removal of my right breast on the 27th. I was surprised to find that these days they don't let you suffer more pain than can be avoided. They use anaesthetics, opiates and sleeping draughts, in fact everything possible to help you. As time goes on it is more than likely that a way will be found to combat cancer and all malignant growths, but in the meantime a way has been found to lessen the pain.

It is my first experience of hospitals and in spite of the reason for being there, I found it most interesting and sometimes amusing. For one thing, the set-times for using bed pans. The nurses would come in with enough pans for the different rooms (mine was a two-bed room) and ask if you wanted a pan: if not, they didn't like it.

When Matron came round, she told me to ring my bell for anything I wanted, so when I needed a pan I rang for it. In would bounce the nurse.

'You refused one when I came round and now you ring for one.'

'Sorry, but I can't manage these things by timetable and Matron told me to ring if I wanted anything, and this is one of the things.'

No more trouble for me, but I heard arguments with the other patient.

...

The Sisters have a way of giving you confidence before the operation. On Monday — I went in Sunday evening — Dr Roland came to see me, asked a few questions and said, 'I'll fix you up tomorrow, Mrs Fitzpatrick. You'll be alright. That do?'

Meekly, I said, 'Thank you, Doctor.'

The day went by, the other patient and I chatted and had our meals. The tea was a very light one for me. I felt nervous, but confident because the patient assured me that she was there during several operations and they all came through safely and didn't suffer as much as they expected.

Next morning at five o'clock, Sister brought me a cup of strong tea and a small slice of bread and butter. At ten o'clock she came with a tray laden with other little trays containing iodine and other things of which I knew nothing.

'I'm sorry it is such a cold day,' she said, 'but I have to prepare you for the surgeon.'

I was stripped to the waist and she began. First sponge and then painting with several kinds of chemical: I thought she would never be finished. She again apologised for the last painting.

'Sorry for this, it is like ice, but you will realise it has to be done for your own sake.'

By the time she had finished putting on my warm bed-sox and lying me on a stretcher, I was past caring.

Going down to the theatre, the Sister took my hand. 'Now don't be afraid,' she said. 'You've got an excellent surgeon and two other Doctors. You are in good hands. Good luck to you.'

On entering the theatre, a voice I knew well as Dr De Garis greeted me. 'I'm here Mrs Fitzpatrick — your own Doctor. You'll be alright.'

And then another voice, 'You won't know me in this mask, but I'm Dr Parker and I saw you yesterday.'

'Yes,' I agreed, as if in a dream. It all seemed so unreal happening to me. I was placed under the big light and a sweet smell began to gently pour around me.

That is all I knew until I found myself back in my bed and it was dark. I was in some kind of trouble but I didn't care. The operation was at eleven o'clock and I was still deep under at seven in the evening, though I knew the different voices of Geoff and Bess, Dad and Dulcie, as if in a dream. Sister came in and gave me a needle as soon as they had gone, and several times during the night and in the morning.

It was a long, long night after the operation. All the feeling I had was for a drink. A Sister came in frequently to wet my lips and let me have one sip only. She was most kind and attentive. They are wonderful if you are really ill, but if you show any signs of getting better, you are treated as if you are quite alright. After a while one longs for home life, but just as I was recovered enough to come home, I caught a chill and had to stay for another fortnight. Pleurisy is no joke.

Dead blowflies can't hurt you

Throughout the 1940s, while Theo was working in Tasmania and then travelling in Europe, we see Ethel and Bert forever out of step with each other. Like the Amazon warrior, allegedly removing her right breast so that she might more easily draw the bow, Ethel, with her right breast surgically removed, soldiers on, enduring an existence she says she would never repeat if she had the choice to do it all again.

24 September 1948

I couldn't have left hospital for another week if Bessie hadn't told the Doctor she would look after me. But, after a fortnight with her, I began to feel a burden and consequently fidgeted to get away. I knew full well that my time for good food and attention was over if I came home. It was plain that I came home to the detriment of myself, but there was no other way.

It is two months since the operation, so I will try and be patient. Not that I am anxious to work or feel fit for it, but because Pop gets in such a muddle and I can't stand it if I can't move about at all. He gives me a dirty cup when I have tea in the morning. This morning it had the marks of tea on the other side from the night before. It really puts me off food at the time I need building up.

Of course he can't understand. Yesterday I made a jug full of orange and lemon drink. When I wanted some, I found two blowflies in it and he saw me throwing it out.

'Good heavens!' he cried. 'Throwing away good stuff like that — the blowflies are dead and can't hurt you.'

Women matter as much as men do at the end of the Queenscliff era

Theo's mother was a prolific writer, and from the beginning her strong persona disturbed my focus on Tasmania. In 2009, when we moved to Point Lonsdale, I volunteered as a local heritage guide. During training I discovered that Ethel Fitzpatrick, whose diaries and letters were stored in my wardrobe, was buried in the cemetery just two blocks away. I began to extend Theo's memoirs to include her Victorian roots, and it was like opening the proverbial Pandora's box — out flew Ethel's voice!

In 2010, we moved a short distance from the Borough of Queenscliffe, through Mannerim to Indented Head, to another townhouse overlooking the water. The scuttled wreck of the Ozone paddle-steamer was in full view of our balcony, with the salvaged anchor not far from our front door, a reminder of the late 1800s when the Ozone was the first luxury paddle-steamer on Port Phillip Bay.

At Indented Head, summer tent cities sprung up overnight like field mushrooms. I pondered the likelihood that I was finishing the Thwaites' story on the very spot the young London couple, Ethel's parents and Theo's grandparents, had pitched their tent in the early 1860s. I watched wave upon wave of bird migration and felt a bond with Mary Ann Thwaites, who'd known all the nuances of my familiar seascape, the woman whose spirit of adventure was shared by her granddaughter Theodora, who took to pitching tents while trekking in Tasmania.

Indented Head was also the place where co-author, Lorraine Secen, came on camping holidays in the 1950s, with her family. 'Memories of a Fisherman's Daughter' was the title of the chapter she contributed to a family history of her father's boat building activities:

> Ours was a very male household. The combination of a father who loved the outdoors, shooting and fishing, who brought up his three sons to be the same, and accompany him on these pursuits made it so. There was really no place for female pursuits in such a household.[4]

Tying together the experiences of three Queenscliff generations of women from the pioneer Thwaites family, with Ethel leaving the Bellarine Peninsula shortly before Theo returned from Europe, made me think of James Stephens' poem *The Shell*. The poet, listening to the timeless sound of a shell, imagines the big picture of the place before there were people, before the earliest animals colonised the land, back to the time when molluscs and cephalopods were evolving:

> It was a sunless strand that never bore
> The footprint of a man

He became aware that the shell would sound the same in a world without people. Ethel's time in Queenscliff cannot be measured against a timeless shell, but in the space where she lived in this pocket of the Bellarine Peninsula, and through her writing, she left a footprint equal to her brother, William J. Thwaites, five times Mayor of Queenscliffe. And like that saying, 'Old soldiers never die, they simply fade away,' this magnificent woman begins to fade out of the picture.

29 October 1948

Father is very worried again over the property at Queenscliff. I do wish he would sell it, or that he had sold it when he had the chance. The present tenant has done what the previous one did: bought out the only other baker there and left our shop, or the premises, keeping the shop alone open. That means he is not using the bakehouse, which will fall into disrepair.

13 February 1949

We've had a peculiar summer here, with alternating blazing days, piercing cold, rain and roaring gales, while Theo tells us that England has had an unusually mild winter. She intends returning home in September this year. I wonder if she will like her own country better for having seen the old land from which so many of our forebears came to make a home here, which was a wilderness in those days. I remember that my parents loved the space, the sunshine and the freedom of the new land, with no past and everything ready to be made anew.

Dad sold the shop at long last and will have no more worry on that score. Got a good price for it really, because not many people like stairs.

The Stresa stationmaster in his office full of roses

Theo loved Italy, both for the people and the art galleries. She travelled to Stresa, Como and Florence, where she said the Piazza del Signoria always left her weak at the knees. Travelling by train in Italy in 2010,

I arrived at Stresa, and remembered Theo's thirty-two page letter mentioning the stationmaster. Here is an extract, with all the *joie de vivre* of Theodora Fitzpatrick, and every young Aussie backpacker on the threshold of their future:

June 1949

The fact that we had a glorious view down the valley didn't assist in getting us a hitch to Simplon, or to Italy. When an occasional car went past it was full up, and anyway the road was very steep and winding. So at about 10.30am we thought we would have to return to Brig and give up our plan of going to Florence and Italy. While we were waiting with about five minutes to go for the bus to come, a car came past, and stopped when we flagged it. It was a French couple on their honeymoon. And where do you think they were going? To Stresa, in Italy! And yes, of course we could come too! It was a magnificent stroke of luck.

The road up to Simplon led through larch forests until it rose above the tree line. The pass is about 6000 feet high and the road goes through tunnels here and there to protect it against avalanches in winter. Right on top of the pass is the statue of an eagle, but oddly lacking in any strength, vitality or real feeling. Since they've performed such marvellous feats with roads, and all sorts of engineering constructions, it's a marvel to me that these Herculean efforts aren't emphasised in this sculpture.

I can't really adequately describe the Simplon Pass — beyond the tower of Simplon, the road swoops down past bare rocks. 'Savage,' as the Frenchman said. Before the town we were among the snow-capped peaks; after the town we were among rocky ravines, and the road precariously built between the hills. Again, of course, a tumultuous stream with waterfalls thundering, or feathering down, into it.

When we finally arrived at Stresa, it was awfully hot and there didn't seem to be a soul about. We said goodbye to our nice French couple and trooped off to the Change Bureau to get some lira. It converted at about 160 lira to one Swiss franc, a pretty good rate. Then we went to the station and the difficulties set in. Everyone spoke Italian, of course. We couldn't get anywhere until one of the porters took us in to the stationmaster. Once again my awful French came to the rescue and we were fixed up in no time. We bought tickets to Firenze, which turns out to be Florence. We parked our rucksacks, said bless you to the stationmaster in his office laden with roses.

We walked up the street, bought a couple of postcards and then sat out on the quay at one of the open-air cafes, and had two ices over a period of three hours and just watched the hills and the water and the boats and the people. Everywhere there was the most wonderful perfume of roses and lime trees and jasmine.

. . .

We caught our train at 10.18 at night, after we'd had a wash under great difficulties at the station. The 3rd class compartment was fairly comfortable, but it was a pretty trying night with only patches of sleep. We were awake at about 5am the next morning and when we weren't passing through tunnels, we were going through hilly country covered with yellow broom and some sort of green growth. Further down there was intense cultivation, with fields of ripe corn and grape vines as far as the eye could see. We arrived at Firenze at 5.55am and it was darned hot. We had a cup of awful Italian coffee and a queer, but interesting, bun and searched for a place where damen only could wash, but it was an unsuccessful search. We decided to find the Youth Hostel and have a clean-up there.

Well we didn't know anything about Florence of course, and we hadn't a map of the city to find our address. I asked a lady if she knew where it was. She spoke only Italian, but in one second flat there were about fifteen people around us all talking madly. One of them could speak French, so he interpreted to the crowd in general. It eventually transpired that the lady to whom I first spoke was going to our very spot. Everybody was terribly happy, the crowd dispersed and we set off with our new guide. We caught a tram to the Youth Hostel and the Warden, or Pere Aubergiste, came out, still in his pyjamas and took our cards. The girls' section of the hostel was an open-air dormitory. Some of the girls were up and some were lying in briefs and bra-tops sunning themselves. We settled ourselves in, had a thoroughly good cold wash and felt refreshed. Then, slightly stunned, we set off to explore Florence.

It didn't take long to find the lovely spots. The Piazza di Signoria made me go weak at the knees. It was extraordinary seeing perfection of Michelangelo's out in the square. We went through the Uffizi Gallery, and the statues and busts were to me the best part of it. When you looked at them they were so perfect you expected them to draw a breath and to step down from the pedestal. You could just imagine how they would speak and act because they were so true to character. Outside the Uffizi Gallery is a rectangle formed by the buildings with recesses for figures. Here we saw the great men of Florence: Galileo, Boccaccio, Petrarca, Dante, Michelangelo, Artem, Cellini, Giotto and Machiavelli.

Our day in Florence went from 6am to 8pm at night. We were so stunned with fatigue at the end of it that we just fell into bed and died. We had intended to spend two days in Firenze but that day denuded us of lira. We didn't have any more Swiss francs to convert and we couldn't cash our traveller's cheques in Italy, so we just had to make a bolt home to Switzerland as fast as we could. This was a great grief to me, as I was completely captivated by the city and by the Italians with whom I got on marvellously well, despite the language problem.

...

Next day we slept late and it was about 9 o'clock before we were on the road. We caught the train. Everybody warns everybody about hitching in Italy, although I haven't met anyone to whom anything unpleasant has happened. We caught the train at 11.45, giving us extra time in the Uffizi. We just caught it by the skin of our teeth. This train wasn't very comfortable and our travelling companions were very quiet. The next one was quite different. Most Italians travel with sandwiches and the odd bottle of wine from which they have the occasional swig. One thing I loved about them was the way, in the cities or trains, they'd stare and stare, and if you smiled they'd joyously smile back. And the most amusing thing was they talked in Italian and I'd talk in English and a delightfully incomprehensible conversation ensued, without anyone knowing what anyone else was saying. They really were fun. We continued by train to Como, hitching to Chiasso and then went to the border to Switzerland. We hitched from there to Lugano, arriving at the latter town at about 10pm.

Theo wrote on a postcard, dated 1 June 1949: 'Hello Family, Arrived in Switzerland yesterday at 6am and since then have mutilated four languages. Spent last night at Berne and tonight I'm in Geneva. Switzerland is really lovely — amazingly like Tasmania.' Here, the Rhone Valley and Zermatt, from which the Matterhorn is usually climbed, were her favourites. In a letter to Nancy she described climbing from Zermatt to the 2042-metre Staffeld, with an easy walk through larch forests, the Alps covered with spring flowers, including brilliant blue gentians and yellow ranunculi. Another day, she had wonderful views going up the 3048-metre Gornergrat by foot instead of via the popular railway. While Zermatt had too many tourists for her liking, she enjoyed the spectacle of goats wearing bells, driven out to pasture at 7.30am and returning at 8pm.

Switzerland had a clean atmosphere because they used hydro power instead of coal. There were the great engineering feats of the Simplon and the St Gotthard passes, where the road takes the heights in python-like bends.

Staying in youth hostels and hitchhiking everywhere, except in Italy, Theo spent the summer of 1949 travelling to Switzerland, Italy, Paris, Land's End, Wales, Eire, Northern Ireland, Scotland again, and the Lake District. She returned to London, where she'd declined an offer of work with a prestigious firm of chartered accountants. At the beginning of August, she commenced a very easy job with the S E Gas Board near Hyde Park Corner. During a one-and-half-hour lunch, she visited art galleries and explored London stores, including Liberty's, Dickens & Jones and Swan & Edgars.

Borough of Queenscliffe wants to know, 'Does Ethel Thwaites' writing have literary merit?'

Theo sent a postcard to her parents of the Inner Harbour in Torquay, England, showing tiers of two- and three-storey buildings. Her parents were now living in the seaside village of Torquay, Australia. Theo wrote:

25 June 1949

This might be the shape of things to come! The English town is very pleasing anyway — 50,000 inhabitants! It reminded me of Stresa in Italy. There are flowers and promenades everywhere — the sands and the cliffs are red, as they are in Devon. And the sea really smelt like the sea, which it usually doesn't over here.

I rifled through boxes, looking for more information. Herbert had sold the shop and the farm, and suddenly they'd moved to Torquay. Ethel was obviously too overwhelmed to write how she felt leaving the Queenscliff vicinity, where she had strong family ties going back to 1858. It remained a story untold — all that *history* and *herstory* was lost.

And then we laughed, when in 2010 our publisher made a formal request for the Borough of Queenscliffe to support this book about three generations of Queenscliff women, and the borough manager requested confirmation that the diaries and letters of Ethel Thwaites, born right there in Queenscliff in 1875, had literary merit.

Swans ringing bells at Wells Cathedral, Somerset

The International Genealogical Index records that John and Mary Ann Thwaites were born in Offulstone (Tower Division), which includes the Parish of Bethnal Green in London, where the couple married on 20

July 1856.[5] Approaching one hundred years later, the youngest of their seventy grandchildren was in the country they left behind and visiting places that would have tugged the couple's heartstrings till the end of their days in Fishermen's Flat, Queenscliff. Theo wrote this message on a postcard of Wells Cathedral, Somerset:

7 July 1949

Dear Mother,

Wells Cathedral was very interesting and unusual. There are swans on the moat surrounding the nearby Bishop's Palace and as you probably know, succeeding generations of swans have for hundreds of years learned to ring a little bell near the drawbridge when they are hungry. The lime trees are flowering down here and the scent is heavenly.

Love, Theo

Chapter 16

Theo

Married on Friday, trapped in the kitchen on Monday

Theo's marriage was a low-key affair, and afterwards the feisty, adventurous Theo dissolved into thin air. The new, switched-off Theo seemed like a fish out of water! Searching for clues as to what Theo thought about her changed circumstances, I found only a puzzling uncharacteristic silent obedience and acceptance. Was her marriage a self-inflicted penance for not being in Australia to support her mother and the family through Ethel's mastectomy? Did she marry to please her mother or her family?

Theo had big dreams for the future. At what point did she abandon her ambitions? Was she crushed by the rejection of her book about women's recreation in the Tasmanian wilderness? She took the manuscript to England and showed it to a male travel author she'd heard of, hoping to get advice and recommendations. This was a great and commendable idea, but writers struggle at the best of times and the hoped-for support didn't eventuate. Apparently there was only enough room for one man on his mountain.

It is significant that Theo's renewed push to find a publisher overseas coincided with her absence during Ethel's health crisis. A most likely scenario is advanced by Hadary and Henderson: 'When you dismiss goals as being unrealistic, you are very likely responding, without even realizing it, to cultural and family expectations of women.'[1]

With questions hanging in the air, I tried afresh to glean further information about Theo's sudden marriage, from her friend and solicitor

Lorraine Secen. She said simply, 'Some people are better off single,' and characteristically faithful to Theo, she didn't elaborate. This comment, and the disturbing trends reported in studies of women's leadership by Hadary and Henderson, set the scene for the sudden change of direction in the life of Theodora Fitzpatrick, a young woman whose expeditions and writing had challenged existing narrow recreational boundaries for women:

> We know from the studies of women's leadership that one of women's strengths is their sensitivity to others' thoughts and feelings. This is what makes women excel at group dynamics and relationship building. On the downside, women are extremely sensitive to others' expectations about the role of women. The problem is that, without realizing it, this awareness influences women to conform to cultural definitions of acceptable behavior and goals for women and the expectations of friends and family.
>
> These expectations often result in self-limitations, which undermine women's self-confidence and lead them to doubt their own potential. They influence the way women behave, the goals women establish, the risks women take, and the way women define success. When women do break with tradition and take on roles that are inconsistent with cultural, organizational, or family expectations, they often feel guilty and start rationalizing their choices to themselves and others.[2]

Theo met her future husband, divorcee Alan Trickett, through mutual friends, while she was working in Melbourne. She hadn't wanted to meet him at all. He was an accountant and she was an accountant, and as she said, she was already working with one hundred other accountants, and that was enough for her. After avoiding him for six months, they finally met. He appeared to have hardly a romantic bone in his body as he planned their wedding day:

Harrietville, Monday 11 January 1954

Theo dearest,

I suggest we get married on a Friday. Find out if there is a five to eight train up on Fridays. I could go down on the 11.30 bus and meet you in Wangaratta about 2.30 and we could then get hitched and come back that night. So perhaps we could tentatively fix the date for Friday the 29th? That still seems too far away. What an awful bother it is even without fuss. Just think what it would be with receptions, flowers, flower girls, bridesmaids and all the trimmings. It's a wonder that anyone does get married. Thank God you don't want a fuss.

All my love dearest,

Alan

Married life in the mining town of Rossarden

At Rossarden, Theo wrote a story about a stray dog called Punch, replacing their dog Nicky, who had vanished without a trace. It is reminiscent of her early Mannerim writing about the arrival of a new kitten in the aftermath of the family losing everything in a house fire. She used the pseudonym Theo Thwaites, and you can definitely feel her heavy heart when you hold the rejection letter from F. W. Cheshire Publishers.

Running to over one hundred pages, the canine title of the manuscript is misleading, as it soon veers away from Punch and becomes autobiographical. However, if you lift out Theo's references to the unique canine character of Punch, the possum dog poised to enrich Australian folklore, what you have left is an account of married life in the mining town of Rossarden.

My new husband — we were married at Wangaratta, on 27 March 1954 — changed accounting jobs shortly afterwards and we moved to Rossarden, a mining town in the North East of Tasmania, where I worked in the office on a part-time basis. The gravel road from Avoca twisted and climbed two and a half thousand feet up the flanks of Ben Lomond, through wattles, gums, dogwoods and a thick undergrowth of low-growing bushes, emerging at a wooden bridge over a little mountain stream alongside the township of Rossarden, where houses were laid out in mathematical squares. Although surrounded by scenic virgin bushland and with an absence of fumes and chemicals from the mine to kill the trees and grass, as in Queenstown, there was hardly a tree to be seen in any street or yard. The stark tree-denuded town had a wonderful unimpeded view of the mountain and it was a crime against Nature to have razed all the trees prior to building the dwellings. Nature, so rhythmical and satisfying to all the senses, had been brutally assaulted by the town planner.

The Mine with the staff houses clustered around it was a mile further on from the township, and our house was amongst these. It was rather large and set in a quite large block with a big handsome gum at the top of a good slope of lawn. Staff houses were built of various surprising materials with the exception of the well-designed Mine Manager's home, which was constructed of brick and timber, with the picture window in the lounge, sited to capture Ben Lomond's buttresses. Our house was clad in corrugated iron, which sounds dreadful, but it was painted cream and looked quite respectable.

One associates silence with such a place, but this was far from the case. As our house was five minutes from the Mine, the noise was diabolical: twenty-four hours a day, Monday to Friday, there was a thunder of motors and the screeches, thumping and grindings of rocks being crushed. At certain times of the day and night, the miners underground did their blasting, which was always preceded by a piercing shriek from a whistle. One of the shafts went right beneath our house, and crockery and glasses rattled in our cupboards. At weekends the peace was idyllic.

Each of the seasons had its strong characteristics in Rossarden, and the winter cold penetrated the whole house, so that to go from the Wonder-heated warmth of the kitchen in the morning to the furthermost rooms was to experience a drop in temperature that was like a slap in the face. Knitting was a winter occupation at Rossarden: one seemed to knit more there, probably because the winters were longer and colder, and there were so many evenings that we spent around the fire. At least once a winter the hot-water taps froze and we learned to leave the cold-water taps on a very slow drip on nights when snow or frost was expected.

Doing the laundry in winter was also formidable: the cold water was so very cold. And sometimes the washing hung on the line for a week, and then had to be brought in three-quarters dry, and laboriously dried off over the fires. Sometimes in a frost the sheets froze stiff, and if the wind stirred them then, even the best material cracked into little splits. Some of the winter frosts lasted for a week, and it was then that the dry-stone wall in front of our house held the frost at its base for the whole of the week. There was usually some snow at Rossarden during the winter, but the top of Ben Lomond wore its white cap well into spring.

With the high altitude, spring was slow to come, and whilst rosebuds appeared in mid-September, they could not come to flower until late November. The garden stayed asleep until mid-November, and then everything got busy at once: hollyhocks, Russel Lupins, Peruvian lilies, Dutch Irises, Lily of the Valley and the raspberries started up from their hibernation. By Christmas everything that was flowering was in full bloom and the Russel Lupins did best of all; there was deep blue, white, pink and variations of all three — the biggest I have ever seen. They did so well and flowered so freely that I made as many beds of them as possible and the cottage looked very gay in the summertime. Raspberries and strawberries were bountiful too, and I made plenty of jam.

It began to dawn on me whilst we were in Rossarden that we were not going to have any children. After medical check-ups, which established that there was no apparent reason for their non-appearance, I was keen to adopt one, or more: Alan was against this for various reasons, amongst which was that we couldn't afford them. This was true enough, but it didn't seem a real barrier to me. We didn't adopt a child, probably because I didn't persist enough.

Unrecognisable Theo, with a view of Ben Lomond

What has become of the former Theodora Fitzpatrick, who forged a path through the Tasmanian wilderness, undeterred by gender stereotypes? Who is this new Theo Trickett, a woman who is apparently satisfied to have a room with a view of Ben Lomond, when less than eight years earlier she was writing confident descriptions of the camaraderie she enjoyed while skiing with the boys on this mountain? In a glimpse of the past, Theo writes:

I spent the weekend on Ben Lomond with perfect weather and snow. I followed the boys about as usual doing the most foolish and daring things and getting along quite well. My boots had lost a metal protector and I had acute binding trouble to begin with, but after I adjusted the bindings I was quite pleased with the results. If only I can wangle a week up there this year I might be able to ski better. And I realise now that one has to adjust bindings personally, in order to fix them.

Actually I got this damned cold because when we came down from the mountain on Sunday night the boys all had car trouble — Harley's starter wouldn't work, Ernest Mills' car was stuck gloriously and firmly in a ditch, and Charlie Smith's car locked somehow. Net result: about an hour-and-a-half messing about in the cold.

Female careers curtailed by marriage and domesticity

The artist Nora Heysen, like Theo, had a promising career until after the Second World War, when she married a doctor specialising in tropical diseases she'd met in New Guinea during her posting as an Australian war artist:

> Now she had a husband, house and garden, and loved all three, she was busy with wifely and domestic duties and art had to find its place. After enjoying a period of increasing career success, the artist now entered a long period of obscurity.[3]

How Theo's dream materialised, then evaporated

In the back of one of Theo's old cash books she penned notes for a speech across the red money columns, followed by eleven closely written pages where she copied the second draft of her mother's family history:

Madam President and Members,

I have been asked to tell you about my visit overseas and will begin by mentioning how this dream of mine materialised. Perhaps, primarily, the urge to do so was reading and becoming interested in the Arts — music, sculpture, architecture, and so on; to see for myself things that could only be dreamed of over here.

In my work in the two states, Victoria and Tasmania — particularly in the latter — in my position as Sub Manager in a firm of accountants over there, I met with many interesting personalities and felt more and more acutely the longing to see other countries, particularly the British Isles, France, Switzerland and Italy.

Now this I knew would be difficult to realise, but I was lucky enough to meet a girl in the office who was interested in joining me. Eventually we did travel together (as a matter-of-fact she is still in England) and we left Melbourne on 8 May 1948 on the *Orion*, really on our way and very thrilled to know the great adventure had begun.

One would think that it would occur to Theo that her qualifications and experience put her on an equal footing with her new husband. But for the remainder of her time in Tasmania, the newly married Theo seemed to lose sight of who she was, and her identity merged with the rather colourless persona of Alan.

The old taboos against the employment of married women,[4] relaxed during World War II, may have been a factor in keeping her housebound, with the 1954 census showing that only thirteen percent of married women were employed.[5] What is certain is that the proud single businesswoman who wrote the speech above was transformed into the dependant married woman who penned the following letter to her mother:

28 July 1954
Dear Mum,

At last I seem to have the time to write: we've been having a hectic time. The previous accountant left things in the most dreadful muddle — every single thing has to be straightened out, and of course the current work goes on all the time. He ran pictures twice a week in the township, kept the books of a couple of stores here and at Storeys Creek and ran the baker's shop. So he apparently just used the job as a source of regular income and made as much as he could on the side.

As for the job, Alan has only had about four nights off since he started: they've mostly been midnight sessions too. I go down in the afternoons and do the typing and Nick takes rather a dim view of being shut in the house. Lately I've been helping Alan a bit at nights, too — it's too big a load for one. We live practically right on the mine — Alan has about two minutes to walk.

I'm glad we live at the end of the township though — it's ugly, not at all like H'ville. The scenery generally isn't a pitch on that lovely valley, except for the lovely ramparts of the Ben. Has it been cold, though! We got a radiator as soon as I came, and I transport that all over the house wherever I'm working. The Wonder-heater in the kitchen is excellent, but it takes a while to light, with the wood all damp.

Nick loves the radiator by the way: it doesn't hiss and crack like a fire, or spurt up with sudden flames. She misjudges the distance, though, and lies with her head nearly in it — she'll catch fire one day! She had a fit of the blues straight after arriving, as if she wondered where we'd be going off to next. Then she found a frightfully disreputable pup called Punch to play with — a ginger and white creature who is a stray — funny ginger eyes, too — and she's been her own happy self ever since.

Theo

Home and family are a woman's domain

Theo, married on a Friday, was trapped in the kitchen on Monday. Francis Crowley writes of the time:

> In a society which held obvious masculinity in high regard, women were neither expected nor encouraged to be active in public life. Home and family were a woman's domain. If she shared the comfort of the period, it was by reducing the drudgery of housework with the new electrical gadgets, and by limiting the size of her family.[6]

Perhaps the reason for the sudden docility and meek demeanour of the formerly feisty Theodora Fitzpatrick was that when girls are in mixed groups, which for Theo can be equated as entering a male-female marriage partnership, they adopt the role or stereotype behaviour they know boys believe is appropriate behaviour for girls, while in contrast the boys' performance doesn't vary in the presence of girls.

Hadary and Henderson explain this as the expectation of males that women should not be risk takers, which is countered by the belief by females that males believe it is inappropriate for women to aspire to maximising rewards. Thus these stereotypes could have potentially become barriers to Theo owning her own destiny, and having the confidence to develop and pursue her former personal goals. [7]

Would Theo Fitzpatrick's opportunities have been different if she'd lived in the twenty-first century? Perhaps not, as according to Hadary and Henderson, many factors continue to conspire to keep women on the other side of the fence:

> Boundaries often are created by those who care about you the most and whom you respect and want to make happy. Your parents, relatives, husbands or partners, friends, and even your children have expectations about what constitutes success for a woman — marriage, children, a clean house, being a good cook, actively

> volunteering for your children's school or your community — and the list goes on. Even today, having a flourishing career often is not part of other people's definitions of success for you. Families expect men to become presidents of their companies or the nation; they expect women to have a 'little' career or start a small hobby business.[8]

Back in 1948, Myra Roper, Principal of University Women's College in Melbourne, believed more British women than Australian women had progressed in advancing their careers on the same terms as men. An apparent lack of feminist solidarity and belief in the rights of both sexes by many Australian women was confirmed as the reason. Moreover, it was Roper's opinion that the shortage of women in Australian public life in 1952 was because 'Australian women do not know how good they are'.[9]

Exactly two decades after Theo's 1954 marriage, The National Women's Conference on Socialism and Feminism was held in Melbourne, with more than 600 women attending. Generally, it was agreed that capitalism and patriarchy created a 'double oppression' for women, both locking them into the 'women's role'. Women were conceptualised as consumers and sex symbols, unpaid workers and sex objects.[10]

Chapter 17

Mary Ann, Ethel and Theo

Lost *herstories* cannot be plucked out of thin air

Making Herstory: Voices of the Thwaites and Fitzpatrick Women Across Time and Place conveys the complexity of female thinking and experience, as it traces the lives of Mary Ann, Ethel and Theo through childhood, youth, middle and old age. As the women voice their aspirations, triumphs and regrets, Ethel in particular questions the relationship of past and present, and the meaning of life itself.

Sifting through these three generations of Australian women, Ethel emerges as the one hell-bent on breaking the stereotype boundaries, with her insistence that Theo gain qualifications to equip her for single, independent life. Initially I had the expectation that the youngest of the female trio was the most likely feminist trailblazer. For a while I lost sight of the foundations built by Mary Ann Thwaites and Ethel Fitzpatrick. I had overlooked the fundamental point that women's freedom comes from the sacrifice of the sisterhood through the ages. That was why we were writing this book — lost *herstories* cannot be plucked out of thin air!

The magnificent Mary Ann, her contribution to Queenscliff enshrined in the writing of daughter Ethel, died in 1913, approaching her seventy-seventh birthday. Her devoted husband John reached eighty-five before he passed away in 1921. Their shared pioneer grave in the Point Lonsdale Cemetery is of great local historical significance.

Queenscliff, with its Victoriana buildings frozen in time, allows Making Herstory to bring pioneer women into the picture. In the small 1868 church, situated in the main street in the heart of the seaside village, the observant child, Ethel Thwaites, recalled details of the congregation and later wrote her engaging descriptions of the people who lived there in the 1880s.

Young Ethel could hardly dream that she would one day play the organ in the new 1888 Wesleyan Church next door, accompanying visiting choirs and celebrated soloists, and much more — she celebrated her wedding here, attended the funerals of her children and the Sunday morning service on her fiftieth wedding anniversary with all her family.

Ethel remains a complex, intelligent woman, denied the opportunity to bloom after a lifetime of running a business while raising a family. After her mastectomy in 1948, Ethel reconnected with her eldest daughter Dulcie Huggins, who was twenty when Theo was born. Dulcie, the mother of two sons — the Fitzpatricks' only grandchildren — was widowed early in her marriage. When Theo married in 1954, her parents were already living at Torquay, and their relationship with Dulcie was blossoming on the neutral sands. The bad memories of growing up in the Queenscliff cake shop were forgotten in the shared joy of the children of their grandson, Winston.

One can imagine Herbert and Ethel Fitzpatrick's pride, as they rediscovered the daughter who had kept them at arm's length while singlehandedly raising her children — Winston, who became an industrial chemist and John, who served in the Royal Australian Air Force from 1941 to 1946.

When Ethel died on 22 August 1958, aged eighty-three years, she had lived to see the one hundred year anniversary of her parents' arrival in Melbourne on 14 August 1858. Furthermore, she had finally been afforded the opportunity to enjoy her family. In one of her last surviving letters to her daughter Theo, her final words, 'too egotistical', seem to echo in the empty chasm of lost *herstories*:

5 July 1949

Nearly three months have passed since my last entry. It seemed that there was nothing to scribble about, tho' I really began this as a relief to

the mind, an outlet, and meant to use it to express my own innermost thoughts. But I have hesitated to do that. So much one thinks about — such as books — when read over, is too egotistical.

Was Ethel Fitzpatrick egotistical? Certainly. And we should applaud this as an admirable quality in a woman living at a time when society typically failed to nurture and grow girlhood ambitions into a respected female identity.

A sisterhood stretching the stereotype boundaries

The female traditions that bind women together can be seen in comparison with the Thwaites and Fitzpatrick women, and the lives of the female writers, musicians and artists of the time. Artist Rosalie Gascoigne is to be admired for breaking through the stereotype barrier: the invisible door that closes on older women. With a meteoric rise, this mature age sculptor and assemblage artist emerged to join the ranks of women who have a tenuous grip on Australian art history. Represented in all major state and national galleries, significant private collections and overseas collections, including the Metropolitan Museum of Art in New York, the untrained Gascoigne began her art career at the age of fifty-seven, when her husband was finishing his, at the Mount Stromlo Observatory in Canberra:

> The first day I decided I could be an artist — a real artist! — I brought home a whole hillside of 30 beautiful old weathered bee boxes I'd found at an abandoned apiary and dumped them in the front driveway. Ben rushed out, totally shocked at my 'dirty old boxes' and proclaimed he'd never seen such obsession. I replied: 'You of all people should understand obsession — you've been staring at the stars in your patch of sky for your entire career! Now it's my turn to be obsessed!'[1]

Gascoigne was one of those rare women who accomplished a feat that should be fundamental to society's expectations of women today. We should expect women to have parallel vocations after raising a family, make allowances for them to be late bloomers and support the endeavours of our mothers, sisters, daughters, nieces and aunties. There should be more recognition that women's lives are put on hold by the circumstances of raising a family. Brooke Fraser's love song *Arithmetic*, in particular the line 'When the years are showing on my face and my strongest days are gone', was stuck in my mind all day. At first it reminded me of Rosalie Gascoigne, but then it prompted the memory of an Elizabeth Jolley book launch.

Australian author Elizabeth Jolley was seventy-four at the 1998 Melbourne launch of her third-last novel, *Lovesong*. Waiting near the end of a long queue for Elizabeth to sign my copy, I told Mark Rubbo, of Readings, that the author's late-in-life success was an inspiration and that I wanted to be like her.

When she died in 2007, Jolley had published fifteen novels, including an autobiographical trilogy, as well as several short story collections and three books of non-fiction.

Rubbo didn't comment one way or the other for five minutes, but then he took me aside and said quietly, 'You cannot be like Elizabeth Jolley; she's one of a kind.' He told me what I already knew. He stressed that she was always a writer and had endured years of rejection, before she was finally published at the ripe old age of fifty-three.

So what of women who've published, composed, painted or done photography prior to having children, who hope to re-join the mainstream? How do they break free of stereotype boundaries they are not consciously aware of, in order to achieve their full potential? If they're blessed with talent and longevity, and destiny is on their side, will success always be the exception rather than the rule? Will the world find new ways to recognise and accommodate the wonderful multifaceted complexity that is woman? What will be women's place and destiny in the twenty-first century?

Theodora Fitzpatrick can be seen as a woman who subverted the stereotype of women's boundaries, until something changed. While her autobiographical stories and letters give clues, it was the 2005 interview conducted by myself and co-author Lorraine Secen, with Theo's Tasmanian friend and climbing companion Nancy Shaw, that provided more valuable insight.

'You continued to do things that Theo seemed unable to do,' Lorraine began. 'In later years, she got bogged down with survival things, like household problems. She just couldn't get out from beneath them.'

'I don't think she was born to be a housewife,' Nancy commented matter-of-factly.

'I think her life seemed to change.' Lorraine was reflective. 'She often said they worked too late. Alan wouldn't retire and she couldn't do some of these things because her life was constrained by the business they ran.'

'She was involved in conservation and religion — mystical things,' said Nancy.

'You were such a lifeline to Theo,' Lorraine complimented Nancy. 'I mean, up until her death, you were a very large part of her life.'

'We arranged a trip in 1994,' said Nancy. 'When we got to Melbourne Airport, there was Theo in a wheelchair!'

'It was the only way we could get her in,' said Lorraine.

'In any respect, it shocked my system,' said Nancy. 'I suppose we couldn't have postponed it?'

Lorraine was surprised. 'You were quite horrified, were you?'

'Of course I was horrified.'

'She hadn't told you that she was in the state she was in?'

'No. And why go ahead? All the time we were at Kakadu she

couldn't do anything. I mean, we went for one little launch trip on a yellow billabong.'

'Yellow Waters,' said Lorraine.

'She hardly went outside. Our cabin not being near the dining room, at first I had to bring her meal down to her.'

'Oh, really?'

'And then she would stagger up with her hand on my shoulder.'

Lorraine seemed ambushed by Nancy. 'You see,' she began. 'I had no idea you didn't know the state she was in — that she hadn't told you. I mean … I wouldn't have been able to get her from the car to the plane without a wheelchair. So that really put a damper on the trip … for you it was almost a disaster. You didn't do anything that you wanted to do?'

'Well, actually, I didn't think you could do much there.'

'Except sit and watch birds. And you were still quite active. This is eleven years ago now. And you were quite amazingly active then.'

Nancy was proud of her stamina. 'From Darwin I joined an Australian Pacific Tour,' she replied. The knee problems evident after Theo's ascent of Frenchman's Cap were a precursor to severe osteoarthritis, and the plucky Nancy had no empathy for her friend's predicament.

Lorraine Secen always had the impression that Ethel never wanted Theo to marry. We can read between the lines of Ethel's letters and see it in the guarded comments about the character of Theo's earlier male friends. We cannot discount that she projected her own unhappy experiences onto her daughter.

It is entirely possible that Theo's dependency on Alan Trickett, her hamstrung behaviour exhibited early in their marriage, was a learned response, the consequence of a patriarchal upbringing. Was marrying in the remote Victorian country town of Wangaratta equivalent to eloping to Gretna Green? Were her elderly parents invited to witness her marriage to divorcee Alan Trickett? Most likely they disapproved, the distance gave them an excuse to stay away, and this was comfortable for all concerned.

When Theo and Alan married in 1954, Theo, a professional woman, found herself relegated to home duties, while Alan took up an accountant's position at the Rossarden mine in Tasmania. The question of whether Theo was satisfied with married life is best judged in the light of the recognition of her accomplishments in Geelong.

It wasn't until they left Tasmania and moved to Victoria that Theo reclaimed her career. The husband and wife set up their own accounting practice, called Centralised Machine Accounting, in Ryrie Street, Geelong, and worked together until they retired in 1970.

Both Lorraine and myself grew up in Geelong. Unlike Ethel and Theodora in nearby Queenscliff, I was unaware that all my great-grandmothers had arrived in sailing ships and walked along the same streets, piers and beaches. Neither did the stories of women from Geelong's early history filter through to me. Knowing about real women who had once been part of my childhood environment would have given me a connection. Instead, I distinctly remember feeling that it was an alien and puzzling place.

Retracing the footsteps of Theodora, the last surviving of the seven children of Ethel and Herbert Fitzpatrick, we find her still in Geelong in 1995, writing to her Tasmanian friend Gwladys. Imagine that for over half a century after she left Tasmania, Theo lived on the flat plain of Geelong, on Corio Bay, against the backdrop of the purple-blue You Yangs that attracted explorer Matthew Flinders to climb them in 1802. Her mind remained focused on climbing, skiing and bushwalking in Tasmania, but her almost eighty-year-old body was letting her down:

30 May 1995
Very dear Gwladys,

There you are heading fast for your 90th birthday and me staggering along to my 80th, if I make it in December! But it is wonderful to remember those magic moments in Tasmania — weren't we fortunate to go to Cradle before it ever became so popular — they speak of 'power walking through the Reserve'! And think of Du Cane, and the Labyrinth, and Rufus, and Ossa, and Ben Lomond and Father Wellington! Think of catching a tram from your house to Lenah Valley terminus and walking up Wellington to the top in one and a half hours — oh, and the satisfaction of that lovely bare shoulder of the mountain and the view from the top.

Fred Smithies knew Weindorfer so well, that he always said of Cradle Mountain, 'So here there is no time, and nothing matters.' I get that release when Alan's away for the weekend.

Yes, the birds still come. Do you want to know the birds we'd see if we could walk down to the river, four doors downhill? After all, we chose to live here, near the river, because of the lovely walks just down at the end of the street. Isn't it ironic! Alan can still walk, but has to have someone with him, but anyway for me the kitchen windows make a wonderful hide.

Living in Geelong, Theo became a regular diarist, as her mother had done in Mannerim. The difference was that she followed the familiar Thwaites theme of birdwatching. She'd left the wilderness of Tasmania to become an accountant, was married to an accountant and, not surprisingly, many of her recorded bird sightings resembled columns of figures. Theo was an active member of the Geelong Field Naturalists Club and she and her brother Bill were involved in the Bird Observers Club project, The Australian Bird Atlas, which started in 1977.

Under Theo's impetus, the Geelong Environment Council was formed in 1972 and she became one of the foundation members. She was the GEC secretary for many years and worked in the office one day a week. For this commitment and her contribution to the environment, enhanced by an extensive knowledge of birds, she was made a life member.

In the last thirty years of her life, she was a passionate birdwatcher, filled twenty-one diaries with observations from her Geelong garden and the nearby Barwon River, from 16 March 1971, until her final entry:

12 December 1997

This morning the Song Thrush, *Turdus philomelos*, started to sing at five past five.

We recognise the bond of enduring mother-daughter love in Ethel not wanting to see Theodora repeating her mistakes, constrained by an unhappy marriage and orthodoxy. Without qualifications it was impossible for Ethel to stand on her own feet, but a further twist in the women's story was that Theo needed more than qualifications to be an independent thinker.

Ethel was unsuccessful in her bid to save her beloved Theo from an almost identical fate. Alan and Theo Trickett's Geelong accountancy firm was equivalent to the burden of Bert and Ethel Fitzpatrick's Queenscliff bakery and cake business. Lorraine Secen was witness to Theo's misery in Geelong, pining for the peaks of Tasmania — a daughter every bit as discontented in her later years as her mother was on the Mannerim farm away from the piers of Queenscliff. Was Theo satisfied with married life? When Alan died she told Lorraine she'd lost the love of her life, and love was something that had appeared to elude her mother Ethel.

In the Point Lonsdale Cemetery, in the Methodist section, two headstones can be found standing in close proximity. One is for John and Mary Ann Thwaites, and the other is for Herbert and Ethel Fitzpatrick, with a memorial attached for their daughter, Theodora Ethel Trickett. It was Theo's request that her ashes to be scattered in a garden — perhaps the Geelong Botanical Gardens, with a small tablet, as a memorial, on her parents' grave at Point Lonsdale near where her grandfather and grandmother Thwaites are buried. Thus the journey of the three women came full circle, beginning and ending in the Borough of Queenscliffe, a place set apart and used for a particular purpose — a place of strategic importance to the fledgling colony.

Écriture féminine: Making *herstory*

The title of this book places it in the *écriture féminine* category. This inspirational term was coined by French feminists to represent an ideal future achievement rather than a particular type of writing. However, as it translates in English to 'women write', the usage can be variable. Elaine Showalter redefined it in 1986, as the inscription of the female body and female differences in language and text.[2]

The book most like *Making Herstory*, in my mind, is Virginia Woolf's 1931 novel *The Waves*, which was conceived in its early stages as the representation of 'a mind thinking', not a sexless or androgynous mind, but the mind of a woman, according to Kate Flint in the book's introduction.[3] Making *herstories* was a recurring theme for Woolf, who also used ideas associated with women's writing to focus on her 1929 book, *A Room of One's Own*, which she wrote after she lectured at Cambridge about the relationship between woman's self-expression and her position within society.[4]

Woolf's thoughts entered the third dimension entirely when she jumped from considering the shape of female thought to an examination of how the female body challenges the writer. In the following dual writing and fishing imagery, Woolf could well be describing the body language of Ethel, the woman born in Fishermen's Flat, writing her journals:

> In 'Professions for Women', which was first read as a paper to the Women's Service League, she pictures for her listeners a girl sitting with pen in hand, and notes that the image that this picture

> brings to mind is that of a fisherman 'lying sunk in dreams on the verge of a deep lake with a rod held out over the water'.[5]

Ethel's diaries reveal the equal partnership of her pioneer parents, a fact overlooked in Queenscliff's historical recollection of events from the 1850s onwards. Who deemed that only the accomplishments of one half of a couple was important? Whom does it serve when history only recorded the deeds of men? We should all be concerned at this lapse of recording because this place, Queenscliff, alongside the entrance to Port Phillip, was the destination, the journey's end, the entry point for the men and women who are the ancestors of many Australians.

Ethel and Theodora lived in a time of patriarchal values, narrow concepts that relegated women to the position of inferior servants, and didn't recognise that men and women think differently. They belonged to generations that were unable to acknowledge that a woman's point of view balanced both marriage and the running of the country. Mary Ann, Ethel and Theodora's story, while unrecorded in history, was handed down in their family. It was a privilege to bring these strong women into the public arena and to showcase the place and destiny of the women of a fine pioneer family, from The Rip at the tip of the Bellarine Peninsula in Victoria, to the peak of Frenchman's Cap in Tasmania.

The stories in this book — in fact all *herstories* are fundamental to every man and woman, boy and girl. The simple reason we have *history* in the school curriculum is that 'a knowledge of the past prevents us making mistakes in the future'. Women's place and destiny in the twenty-first century is to have equal representation in history books, parliament, boardrooms, the media and the top echelons of industry and professions. Women cannot expect to make gains in the future unless they challenge and correct the patriarchal version of history that continues to be promoted in places of education.

We live in a society that is hungry to seek out and promote the great *herstories* of the world. It is important we reflect on this, and work together to foster and advocate the equal reporting of men and women's sporting, cultural, political, academic or other achievements. Woolf's picture of a man and a woman dreaming in unison — the girl sitting with a pen in her hand, looking like a replica of the fisherman with the rod held out over the water[6] — like two sides of a coin, is symbolic of the emerging voices of several generations of the seafaring Thwaites and Fitzpatrick family, working together towards making *herstory*.

Family and Associates

John Thwaites and Mary Ann Thwaites (nee Martin)

John was born in January 1836 (exact date unknown) and died on 16 January 1921.

Mary Ann was born on 21 November 1837 and died on 5 September 1913.

The International Genealogical Index records that both were born in Offulstone (Tower Division), which includes the Parish of Bethnal Green in London, where the couple married on 20 July 1856. They lived in the English county of Middlesex.

John and Mary Ann Thwaites emigrated from the UK in 1858 with their baby son, John Richard, who died at sea on 25 May 1858. They are recorded on the passenger list of the vessel *Africa* which sailed from Liverpool, England on 16 April 1858, and arrived in Melbourne on 14 August 1858. John was then 23 years old and Mary Ann was 21. Both could read and write. Their religion is not given as Church of England, Roman Catholic or Presbyterian, but of being 'Other Persuasion'. The passenger list records them as going to Geelong on 19 August. From Geelong they moved on to Queenscliff, where they remained for the rest of their lives. Their stay in Geelong could not have been very long, for they had nine more children, all born in Queenscliff between 1861 and 1877.[1]

Their children included six girls, Eleanor Elizabeth, Alice Annie, Isabella, Mary Ann, Ethel and Harriet Eva, and three surviving boys, Alfred, William John and James. Theodora was the youngest of their seventy grandchildren. They have a pioneer grave in the Methodist section of Point Lonsdale Cemetery.

John Thwaites was one of Queenscliff's earliest pioneer fishermen, and he built a cottage off Gellibrand Street in 1870. Rate Books first record him as a fisherman living at the Fishermen's Reserve, owned by The Crown on 2 March 1875. In all subsequent references, from 8 February 1877 to 31 December 1910, his occupation is 'Fisherman', the property owner is 'The Crown' and the property is referred to as 'Cottage Wharf Street'.

John Richard Thwaites 1858

First born child of John and Mary Ann Thwaites.

Born late 1857, or early 1858; died on voyage to Australia on 25 May 1858.

Eleanor Elizabeth Hurford (nee Thwaites) 1858–1934

Eldest surviving and second child of John and Mary Ann Thwaites.

Eleanor was 18 when the last of her ten siblings was born.

At age 21 she married John Hurford on 10 June 1880. They had ten children between 1883 and 1903.

Alfred Thwaites 1861–1922

Third child and eldest surviving son of John and Mary Ann Thwaites.

Married Susannah Wiffen on 25 December 1882. They had seven children: six sons followed by a daughter.

A long-serving Queenscliff boatman, he started in the 1870s and gave forty years of service.

A fisherman, boatman and diarist, Alf is often quoted by Barry Hill in *The Enduring Rip: A History of Queenscliff*.

Rate Books examined from 20 February 1885 to 31 December 1910 record Alf's continuous occupation as a fisherman, with a cottage in Wharf Street on Crown Land.

Thomas Thwaites 1886–1970

Alf's son and Theo's first cousin, Tom started as a boatman in 1911 and responded to the Queenscliff wreck bell for forty-two years.

Alice Annie Eades (nee Thwaites) 1863–1939

Fourth child and second daughter of John and Mary Ann Thwaites.

Married Henry Eades on 6 November 1883. They had eleven children.

Isabella Galbraith (nee Thwaites) 1866–1951

Fifth child and third daughter of John and Mary Ann Thwaites.

Married Alexander Galbraith on 15 July 1890 in a double wedding with Mary. They had six children.

William John (Jack) Thwaites 1868–1929

Sixth child and third son of John and Mary Ann Thwaites.

Married Amy Ann Wiffen on 10 December 1890. They had ten children.

Occupation: fisherman and baker.

Original Thwaites Bakery was at 67–69 Hesse Street. Photo in the Queenscliffe Historical Museum, 49 Hesse Street, Queenscliff.

Served five terms as Mayor of Queenscliffe, in 1910 and from 1916–19.

Mary Ann James (nee Thwaites) 1871–1954

Seventh child and fourth daughter of John and Mary Ann Thwaites.

Married Frederick James on 15 July 1890 in a double wedding with Bella. They had seven children.

James Thwaites 1873–1964

Eighth child and fourth son of John and Mary Ann Thwaites.

Married Alice Germaine on 21 December 1898. They had five children.

Ethel Fitzpatrick (nee Thwaites) 1875–1958

Ninth and second-youngest of the children of John and Mary Ann Thwaites.

Born in Queenscliff on 31 July 1875, died 22 August 1958, aged 83 years. Married on 29 November 1893. Herbert was 23 and Ethel was 18.

Their seven children included Dulcie, Herbert, Mavis, Harold, Geoffrey, Bill and Theodora Ethel. All except Dulcie were childless.

Ethel's writing includes two unpublished novellas: *Life* and *Upheaval*, the latter with a missing ending; three short stories, 'Women', 'A Sketch' and 'Recuperating in the Country'; three 1940s diaries, two versions of Thwaites family and Queenscliff recollections, and a collection of letters.

Buried close by the pioneer grave of her parents at Point Lonsdale Cemetery, also known as the Queenscliff Cemetery, with a memorial to Theodora on the headstone.

Herbert Arthur Fitzpatrick 1870–1956

Theo's father, born in Carlton on 14 February 1870, died on 21 November 1956, aged 86 years.

Occupation: baker and farmer.

Opened Point Lonsdale's first shop in 1901.[2]

Christine Westhorpe Fitzpatrick (birth and death date unknown)

Scottish mother of Herbert Fitzpatrick, and Theodora's paternal grandmother.

Harriet Eva Robson (nee Thwaites) 1887–1952

Tenth and youngest of the children of John and Mary Ann Thwaites.

Occupation: 1897 Queenscliff business directory, Harriet Thwaites, Hesse Street draper.

Married George Henry Robson on 6 October 1897. They had seven children.

Dulcie Naomi Huggins (nee Fitzpatrick) 1895–1984

Theo's eldest sister.

Married Colin Gordon Charles Huggins. They had two sons, the only grandchildren of Herbert and Ethel Fitzpatrick.

Colin Winston Huggins 1919–2009

Eldest son of Colin and Dulcie Huggins.

Occupation: industrial chemist.

Married Carleen Clara Taylor. They had three children.

John Robert Huggins 1921–73

Second son of Colin and Dulcie Huggins.

Occupation: RAAF 1941–46

Unmarried.

Mabel Mavis Fitzpatrick 1902–20

Theo's second-eldest sister.

James Harold Fitzpatrick 1904–19

Theo's second-eldest brother.

Geoffrey Fitzpatrick 1907–72

Theo's third-eldest brother, married to Bessie (surname unknown).

Edgar (Bill) Westhorpe Fitzpatrick 1910–81

Theo's fourth-eldest brother.

Occupation: secondary teacher. B.Sc., Dip. Ed., B.A., conferred 5 August 1957 at the University of Melbourne.

Unmarried.

Ashes scattered in the Labyrinth, Tasmania, by Launceston Walking Club on 24 April 1982.

Theodora Ethel Trickett (nee Fitzpatrick) 1915–98

Youngest child of Herbert and Ethel. Born at Queenscliff on 20 December 1915, when Ethel was 41.

Theodora grew up to become an unconventional bushwalker, mountaineer, naturalist, birdwatcher, writer and poet. She was a young woman with an unquenchable spirit of adventure that saw her hiking in Tasmania and Europe in the 1940s. In the winter, she and fellow skiers would climb Tasmania's Ben Lomond, carrying their skis and provisions to Summit Hut to camp and ski, and during summer she hiked up Ben Lomond. Travelled Europe, leaving Australia in May 1948 and returning in November 1949. Under Theo's impetus, the Geelong Environmental Council was formed in 1972, and she was one of the foundation members.

Married forty-three years to Alan Trickett, a divorcee, at Wangaratta on 27 March 1954.

Occupation: accountant.

Died in Geelong on 2 January 1998, aged 82 years.

Alan Douglas Trickett 1909–97

Theo's husband Alan and twin sister, Constance, were born at St Anne's on the Sea in Lancashire, England on 13 January 1909. Brothers were Ron and Harry.

Occupation: accountant at the mines in Harrietville, Victoria and Rossarden, Tasmania and then in Geelong, where Theo and Alan set up their own accounting practice, Centralised Machine Accounting, in Ryrie Street, Geelong, where they worked together until they retired in 1970.

Died in Geelong on 17 September 1997, aged 88 years.

Thomas Howard Fellows 1822–78

Politician and judge, active in law reform in Victoria in the nineteenth century.

In 1860 he built 'El Tambo' (now called 'Warringah') in Mercer Street, Queenscliff, as his summer home, and John Thwaites was the gardener for an unspecified period.

Among the posts he held were Attorney General and Solicitor General, Postmaster General 1863–64, Leader of the Opposition in Council 1864–68, Minister of Justice and Leader of the Government in Assembly 1868, fifth judge of the Supreme Court 1872, Prahran Councillor 1861–64, Borough of Queenscliffe Councillor 1863–73, Mayor of Queenscliffe 1865.[3]

Marie (Mary) Richardson (nee Bailey) 1835–96 and Ethel Florence Lindesay (Henry Handel) Richardson 1870–1946

Henry Handel Richardson's father was Dr Walter Richardson. He graduated from Edinburgh Medical School, arrived in Melbourne in 1952 and went to the Ballarat gold diggings. He married Mary Bailey after opening Richardson's General Store in Geelong, bought mining shares and struck it rich. Ethel (Ettie) was born while they were living in the Melbourne suburb of Fitzroy. They moved to Chapel Street, St Kilda, when Ada Lillian (Lil) arrived. Walter retired, and was on a grand European tour with his family when New North Clunes Mining Company and his finances crashed. In his fifties, he bought land and built a home in Burwood Road, Hawthorn, where he had an unsuccessful practice.

1876, Ettie was six and Lil was five when her father's general practice in Chiltern failed.

1877, Ettie was seven when Walter became Quarantine Officer at Queenscliff.

1879, Walter died when Ettie was nine and her mother Mary, with little education and without Government social security for widows with children, worked to support and educate her daughters in postmistress positions at Koroit, Maldon and Richmond.

1883, Ettie commenced Presbyterian Ladies College.

1887, Ettie turned seventeen. Final year at PLC.

1888, Mary Richardson sold the formerly unsaleable Hawthorn house for a good sum and resigned from the postal service.

1891, George Robertson and Ethel Richardson announced their engagement.

1895, Ettie was married at the Church of St John the Baptiste in Contarf, Dublin, her father's birthplace.

1896, Mary Richardson died suddenly.

1908, Heinemann published *Maurice Guest* under the masculine pseudonym 'Henry Handel Richardson'.

1917, Heinemann published *The Fortunes of Richard Mahoney*, the first novel in a trilogy now called *Australia Felix*.

1925, Heinemann published *The Way Home*, second novel.

1929, Heinemann published *Ultima Thule*, third novel.

1932, Henry Handel Richardson was one of the first women nominated for a Nobel Prize for Literature. The prize went to a male author.

1933, Ettie's husband, George, died suddenly of cancer.

1948, Heinemann published *The End of Childhood*.

Mona Allen (nee Frawlay) (birth date unknown)

Travelled with Theo to England.

Died on 26 December 1989 in her eightieth year.

Gwladys Morris (birth and death date unknown)

Tasmanian walking companion of Bill and Theo Fitzpatrick.

Unmarried.

Lived in Hobart.

Frederick Smithies (OBE) 1885–1979

Born in Ulverstone on 16 August 1885. Died in Launceston on 13 October 1979.

Lived at 'The Grange' in St Leonards, Tasmania.

Occupation: South Brisbane Insurance Co. in Hobart in 1902, transferring to their Launceston branch in 1908. In 1912 he was appointed manager of the Launceston branch of Atlas Assurance Co., a position he held until his retirement, setting a record of fifty years as manager of the company.

His contribution to bushwalking, exploration, conservation and photography made him a prominent identity in Tasmania for many decades. In 1936, he was in charge of a Tasmanian photographic display at the Melbourne Centenary Celebrations, including Cradle Mountain, that put the Tasmanian wilderness on the map as a tourist destination. The Tasmanian Archives retain Frederick Smithies' original negative collection, a selection of his lantern slides and original prints relating to the early history of bushwalking, skiing and the development of Tasmanian scenic reserves, especially the Cradle Mountain-Lake St Clair National Park.

Rosaline Stephensen (Steve) (birth and death date unknown)

Born in Maryborough, Queensland and grew up in Biggenden.

Lived in Tasmania for thirty-one years.

Occupation: accountant.

Tasmanian walking companion of Theo.

Hobart Walking Club member around 1935, until she left Tasmania in 1966.

Joined Gold Coast Bushwalking Club soon after it started in 1975, was a life member.

Featured in the National Museum of Australia, People and the Environment Interview, 28 January 1993: *Women's bushwalking and outdoor activities: How women have changed in what used to be male dominated sports interests from 1920–1950, such as bushwalking and skiing.*[4]

Nancy Weaver (nee Shaw) 1910–2013

Born on 22 February 1910. Died 22 April 2013, aged 103 years.

Graduated University of Tasmania, B.A. 1932.

Bushwalking and lifelong friend of Theo.

Married Joe Weaver in 1949. Joe died on 17 December 1991. They had one child, daughter Helen, when Nancy was 45.

Interviewed by Helen Downey and Lorraine Secen in her Hobart home in 2005, aged 95 years.

Celebrated her 100th birthday in Hobart in 2010.

One of three centenarian UTAS alumni women to graduate in the 1930s, who were all life members of the Hobart Walking Club and were celebrated with a special morning hosted by Vice-Chancellor Daryl Le Grew, in October 2010.[5]

Mac and Cecily Woodroffe (birth and death date unknown)

Tasmanian walking companions of Theo.

Edward Byam Wight (birth and death date unknown)

Lived at 'The Ridge', 68 Mercer Street in Queenscliff, for forty years.

Wight family occupied 'The Ridge' for eighty-six years.

Mayor of Essendon in 1862. Merchant and partner in early colonial firm, Watson and Wight.

John Thwaites was his gardener.

William Oliver (birth and death date unknown)

Lived in Mercer Street.

Listed as 'a gentleman'.

John Thwaites was his gardener.

Mr Trathan (birth and death date unknown)

Queenscliff State School teacher.

Mr Streeton resigned towards the end of 1878 and Mr Trathan took over as headteacher. Possibly acting headteacher before that time. Variously referred to as headmaster, headteacher and teacher. Took part in church choir singing at that time.

Teacher of Ethel and William Thwaites.

Endnotes

Introduction

1 Anne Longmire, *The Catalysts: Change and Continuity, 1910–2010*, Australia: Anne Longmire and The Catalysts, 2011, p. 184.
2 Sharon Hadary and Laura Henderson, *How Women Lead: 8 Essential Strategies Successful Women Know*, New York: McGraw-Hill, p. 2013, p. 176.
3 ibid, p. xx.

Chapter 1: Mary Ann and Ethel: There were women on the piers

1 Borough of Queenscliffe Rate Book 1863–84, 2 March 1875, No. 270.
2 John W. Allison, 'The Queenscliff Fishermen's Reserve and Its Early Occupants, Parts one, two and three', Document 2364, Queenscliffe Historical Museum, 2008.
3 Francis Keble Crowley, *A New History of Australia*, Buxton, 1870–90; Heinemann, Australia, 1974, p. 185.
4 ibid, p. 205.
5 ibid, p. 206.
6 *Great News Stories of Queenscliff*, '1870s, Pilot schooner hit by big seas — four die', Queenscliff: Queenscliffe Herald, pp. 7–8.

Chapter 2: Ethel: Living in Queenscliff when feminism was a luxury

1 Frances Devlin-Glass and Annette Comte, *Flying 'In Between': Literature and Feminist Theory Since 'Frankenstein'*, Geelong: Deakin University, 1997, p. 38.
2 Anne Longmire, *The Catalysts: Change and Continuity, 1910–2010*, Australia: Anne Longmire and The Catalysts, 2011, p. 4.
3 Borough of Queenscliffe Rate Book 1885–54, 23 February 1892, No. 401; 6 February 1894, No. 404; 31 December 1895, No. 407 and Borough of Queenscliffe Rate Book 1895–1910, 31 December 1896, Nos. 405 and 31; December 1897, No. 405.
4 Borough of Queenscliffe Rate Book 1895–1910, 31 December 1896, No. 38.
5 ibid, 31 December 1897, No. 27.
6 ibid, 31 December 1910, Nos. 25 and 82.
7 Marilyn Lake, *Getting Equal: The History of Australian Feminism*, Australia: Allen & Unwin, 1999, p. 31.
8 ibid.
9 ibid.
10 Discover Mornington Peninsula, 'Fascinating Historic Facts: Mornington Peninsula Paddle Steamers of Port Philip Bay', www.discovermorningtonpeninsula.com.au/fascinatingfacts/paddle-steamers.php.
11 ibid.

Chapter 3: Ethel: Silencing Fish Wives — women can't sing, paint, write or think

1 Silvia Dropulich, 'Silencing Women', *Voice*, *The Age*, July 2010, p. 7.
2 Joanna Fitch, *Beyond the Garden Gate: Local insight into the Victorian female suffrage movement*, Australia: Victorian Women's Trust, 2009, p. 81.
3 ibid, p. 61.
4 ibid, p. 39.
5 ibid, p. 42.
6 ibid, p. 65.
7 Anne Longmire, *The Catalysts: Change and Continuity, 1910–2010*, Australia: Anne Longmire and The Catalysts, 2011, p. 56.
8 ibid, pp. 58–59.

Chapter 4: Ethel: Tyranny and humiliation in Fitzpatrick's Bakery

1 Queenscliff Museum document, unpublished.
2 *Hotels and Guesthouses of Queenscliffe*, 'Boom Era Hotels', Queenscliff: Queenscliffe Herald, pp. 4–5.
3 Marilyn Lake, *Getting Equal: The History of Australian Feminism*, Australia: Allen & Unwin, 1999, p. 23.
4 Borough of Queenscliffe Rate Book, 1895–1910, 1896, No. 38; 1898, No. 39; 1899, No. 39; 1900, No. 39; 1903, No. 45 and 1904, No. 44.
5 Marilyn Lake, *Getting Equal: The History of Australian Feminism*, Australia: Allen & Unwin, 1999, p. 278.
6 ibid, p. 87.
7 ibid, p. 88.
8 Henry Handel Richardson, *Myself When Young*, Great Britain: William Heinemann, 1948, p. 6.
9 ibid, p. 12.
10 'Elegance in Wood', Queenscliff Diary, Victoria: Ministry of Planning and Environment, 1988.
11 Susanna De Vries, *Great Australian Women From Federation to Freedom*. Australia: Harper Collins, 2001, p. 221.
12 ibid, p. 264.
13 Henry Handel Richardson, *Ultima Thule*, Australia: Penguin Books, 1971, p. 125–126.
14 Henry Handel Richardson, *Myself When Young*, Great Britain: William Heinemann, 1948, p. 21.
15 ibid, p. 8.
16 ibid, p. 43.
17 ibid, p. 18.
18 Susanna De Vries, *Great Australian Women From Federation to Freedom*, p. 239.

Chapter 5: Theo: Adolescence on the Bellarine Peninsula

1 *The Sentinel*, 1882–1919, Queenscliff, p. 177.

2 Queenscliffe Urban Conservation Study, The Ministry for Planning Victoria, Geelong Regional Commission, Allom, Lovell & Associates Pty. Ltd. Architects, Reference No. 98, p. 179.
3 Borough of Queenscliffe Rate Book, 10 December 1923, No. 61.
4 Melissa Benn, *What Should We Tell Our Daughters? The Pleasures and Pressures of Growing Up Female*, John Murray Publishers, United Kingdom: Hachette, 2013, p. 29.

Chapter 6: Ethel: In her wildest dreams, she never imagined Theo's independence

1 Melissa Benn, *What Should We Tell Our Daughters? The Pleasures and Pressures of Growing Up Female*, John Murray Publishers, United Kingdom: Hachette, 2013, p. 5.
2 Francis Keble Crowley, *A New History of Australia*, Australia: Heinemann, 1974. pp. 395–396.
3 Ian Wynd, 'Mannerim', *Balla-wein: A History of the Shire of Bellarine*, Victoria: The Council of the Shire of Bellarine, 1988, p. 110.
4 Anne Longmire, *The Catalysts: Change and Continuity, 1910–2010*, Australia: Anne Longmire and The Catalysts, 2011, p. 42.

Chapter 7: Theo: Women climbing Cradle

1 Frederick Smithies, 'Skyline Climb on Cradle Mountain', *The Examiner Annual*, Tasmania, 1937.
2 Diana Holmes and Carrie Tarr, *A 'Belle Epoque'? Women in French Society and Culture 1890–1914*, New York: Berghahn Books, 2006, p. 14.
3 ibid, p. 3.
4 Sally Schnackenberg, *Kate Weindorfer: The Woman Behind the Man on the Mountain*, Tasmania: Regal Publications, 1995, pp. 47–49.
5 ibid, pp. xv–xvi.
6 Diana Holmes and Carrie Tarr, *A 'Belle Epoque'?*, pp. 14–15.
7 Marilyn Lake, *Getting Equal: The History of Australian Feminism*, Australia: Allen & Unwin, 1999, p. 37.
8 Melissa Benn, *What Should We Tell Our Daughters? The Pleasures and Pressures of Growing Up Female*, John Murray Publishers, United Kingdom: Hachette, 2013, p. 20.

Chapter 8: Theo: Independence and freedom, roaming on a bicycle

1 Diana Holmes and Carrie Tarr, *A 'Belle Epoque'? Women in French Society and Culture 1890–1914*, New York: Berghahn Books, 2006, p. 85.
2 ibid.
3 ibid, p. 87.

Chapter 9: Ethel: Rejecting the submissive role patriarchy reserved for her

1 Toril Moi, *Sexual Textual Politics*, London: Routledge, 1985, p. 58.

2 Melissa Benn, *What Should We Tell Our Daughters? The Pleasures and Pressures of Growing Up Female*, John Murray Publishers, United Kingdom: Hachette, 2013, p. 238.
3 ibid, p. 238.
4 Phillip Knightley, *Australia*, London: Jonathan Cape, 2000, p. 37.
5 Henry Handel Richardson, *Myself When Young*, Great Britain: William Heinemann, 1948, p. 51.
6 Jahan Ramazani, *Poetry of Mourning: The Elegy from Hardy to Heaney*, Chicago: University of Chicago Press, 1994, pp. 11–15.

Chapter 10: Theo and Ethel: WWII and the composing genius of Bach and Sutherland

1 Anne Longmire, *The Catalysts: Change and Continuity, 1910–2010*, Australia: Anne Longmire and The Catalysts, 2011, p. 60.
2 Carolyn A. Durham, *The Contexture of Feminism, Marie Cardinal and Multicultural Literacy*, USA: University of Illinois Press, 1992, p. 45.
3 Naomi Wolf, *Fire With Fire: The New Female Power And How It Will Change the 21st Century*, London: Chatto & Windus, 1993, p. 290.

Chapter 11: Theo: Diverse WWII recreational and cultural pastimes for women

1 Anne Longmire, *The Catalysts: Change and Continuity, 1910–2010*, Australia: Anne Longmire and The Catalysts, 2011, p. 61.
2 Francis Keble Crowley, *A New History of Australia*, Buxton, 1870–90; Heinemann, Australia, 1974, pp. 324–325.

Chapter 12: Ethel: Economic independence for all women

1 Marilyn Lake, *Getting Equal: The History of Australian Feminism*, Australia: Allen & Unwin, 1999, p. 91.
2 ibid, p. 201.
3 Melissa Benn, *What Should We Tell Our Daughters? The Pleasures and Pressures of Growing Up Female*, John Murray Publishers, United Kingdom: Hachette, 2013, p. 238.
4 ibid, p. 228.
5 ibid, p. 228.
6 Phillip Knightley, *Australia*, London: Jonathan Cape, 2000, p. 222.

Chapter 13: Theodora, Nancy and Rosaline: There were women on the peaks!

1 Sarah Waight, 'Women's bushwalking and outdoor activities', Rosaline Stephensen interview, National Museum of Australia, 28 January 1993.

Chapter 14: Theo: History required the invisibility of women

1 Marilyn Lake, *Getting Equal: The History of Australian Feminism*, Australia: Allen & Unwin, 1999, p. 6.

2 Sharon Hadary and Laura Henderson, *How Women Lead: 8 Essential Strategies Successful Women Know*, New York: McGraw-Hill, p. 2013, p. 17.
3 Naomi Wolf, *Fire With Fire: The New Female Power And How It Will Change the 21st Century*, London: Chatto & Windus, 1993, p. 85.
4 Janet Hawley, *Artists in Conversation*, Richmond, Victoria: The Slattery Media Group Pty. Ltd., 2012, p. 83.
5 ibid, p. 87.
6 ibid, p. 84.
7 ibid, p. 87.
8 Frederick Smithies, 'Rugged Crags, Nature's Challenge to the Mountaineer', *The Examiner Annual*, Launceston, Tasmania, 1935.
9 Sir William Crowther, 'Biographical Notes for the Frederick Smithies Exhibition', Tasmania: State Library of Tasmania, 1977, p. 5.
10 ibid, p. 6.
11 ibid, p. 7.
12 Marilyn Lake, *Getting Equal: The History of Australian Feminism*, Australia: Allen & Unwin, 1999, p. 198.
13 ibid, p. 188.

Chapter 15: Ethel and Theo: Women's experiences matter

1 Naomi Wolf, *Fire With Fire: The New Female Power And How It Will Change the 21st Century*, London: Chatto & Windus, 1993, p. 119.
2 ibid, p. 122.
3 ibid, p. 150–151.
4 Patrick Grinter, *I Build Boats*, Queensland: Zipprint, 2005, p. 116.
5 John W. Allison, 'The Queenscliff Fishermen's Reserve and Its Early Occupants, Parts one, two and three', Document 2364, Queenscliffe Historical Museum, 2008.

Chapter 16: Theo: Married on Friday, trapped in the kitchen on Monday

1 Sharon Hadary and Laura Henderson, *How Women Lead: 8 Essential Strategies Successful Women Know*, New York: McGraw-Hill, p. 2013, pp. 17–18.
2 ibid.
3 Janet Hawley, *Artists in Conversation*, Richmond, Victoria: The Slattery Media Group Pty. Ltd., 2012, p. 88.
4 Francis Keble Crowley, *A New History of Australia*, Buxton, 1870–90; Heinemann, Australia, 1974, p. 466.
5 ibid, p. 541.
6 ibid, p. 395.
7 Sharon Hadary and Laura Henderson, *How Women Lead: 8 Essential Strategies Successful Women Know*, New York: McGraw-Hill, p. 2013, p. 20.
8 ibid, p. 20.
9 Anne Longmire, *The Catalysts: Change and Continuity, 1910–2010*, Australia: Anne Longmire and The Catalysts, 2011, pp. 145–146.

10 Marilyn Lake, *Getting Equal: The History of Australian Feminism*, Australia: Allen & Unwin, 1999, p. 236.

Chapter 17: Mary Ann, Ethel and Theo: Lost *herstories* cannot be plucked out of thin air

1 Marilyn Lake, *Getting Equal: The History of Australian Feminism*, Australia: Allen & Unwin, 1999, p. 181.

2 Jeremy Hawthorn, *A Concise Glossary of Contemporary Literary Terms*, Second Edition, Arnold, London, 1994, p. 56.

3 Kate Flint, 'Introduction' and 'Notes' in *The Waves*, by Virginia Woolf, 1932, England: Penguin Books, 1992, p. xix.

4 ibid, pp. xviii–xix.

5 Jeremy Hawthorn, *A Concise Glossary of Contemporary Literary Terms*, Second Edition, Arnold, London, 1994, p. 57.

6 ibid, p. 57.

Family and Associates

1 John W. Allison, 'The Queenscliff Fishermen's Reserve and Its Early Occupants, Parts one, two and three', Document 2364, Queenscliffe Historical Museum, 2008.

2 Queenscliffe Urban Conservation Study, The Ministry for Planning Victoria, Geelong Regional Commission, Allom, Lovell & Associates Pty. Ltd. Architects, Reference No. 98, 1982, p. 179.

3 Victorian Heritage Database, www.vhd.heritage.vic.gov.au/places/heritage/4826

4 Sarah Waight, 'Women's bushwalking and outdoor activities', Rosaline Stephensen interview, National Museum of Australia, 28 January 1993.

5 Rhonda Ewart and Janette Brennan, 'Golden girls. A celebration of our centenarian alumni', *Alumni News*. Australia: UTAS, December 2010, pp. 4–5.

Bibliography

Unpublished letters, diaries, memoirs, short stories and transcripts

Downey, Helen. Transcript of recorded Nancy Weaver (nee Shaw). Interview with Helen Downey and Lorraine Secen. Hobart: 2005.

Fitzpatrick, Ethel. Diaries 1941–1949, vol. 1, 2, 3. 24 and 26 January 1941; 6 and 21 February 1941; 14, 17 and 24 March 1941; 5 June and 8 November 1941. 10, 16 and 24 February 1942; 10 March 1942; 6 and 8 April 1942 and 11 and 24 May 1942. 30 October and 12 December 1943. 14, 15 and 18 January 1944; 12 and 14 February 1944; 17 April and 31 July 1944; 27 March 1946. 20 July 1948; 17 and 24 September and 29 October 1948. 13 February and 5 July 1949.

Fitzpatrick, Ethel. Letters to Theo. 8 October 1936; 14 July 1937; 17 April and 7 July 1944; 13 February 1945; 30 April and 15 September 1946; and six undated letter extracts.

Fitzpatrick, Ethel. 'Life in the Early Days: a Queenscliff memoir'. Drafts 1 and 2. Date unknown.

Fitzpatrick, Ethel. 'Recuperating in the Country'. Unpublished. Date unknown.

Fitzpatrick, Theodora. Letters to family and friends. 28 May 1946; 6, 15, 24 and 30 June 1946; 25 June 1949; 7 July 1949; 14 and 26 August 1949; 28 July 1954, to Mother; 30 May 1995, to Gwladys Morris.

Fitzpatrick, Theodora. 'Liebchen'. A teenage memoir. 1932.

Shaw, Nancy. Letter to Theo. 1946.

Stephensen, Rosaline (Steve). Letter to Theo. 1984.

Trickett, Alan. Letter to Theo. 1954.

Trickett, Theodora (nee Fitzpatrick). 'A Dog called Punch'. A Rossarden memoir. 1954.

Trickett, Theodora (nee Fitzpatrick). Twenty-one bird observation diaries. 1971–97.

Trickett, Theodora (nee Fitzpatrick). Final Request. 1994.

Trickett, Theodora (nee Fitzpatrick). Speech notes in Cash Book. Date unknown.

Books, booklets and articles

Allison, John W. 'The Queenscliff Fishermen's Reserve and Its Early Occupants, Parts one, two and three'. Document 2364. Queenscliffe Historical Museum, 2008.

Benn, Melissa. *What Should We Tell Our Daughters? The Pleasures and Pressures of Growing Up Female*. John Murray Publishers, United Kingdom: Hachette, 2013.

Borough of Queenscliffe Rate Books. 1863–84; 1885–94; 1895–1910; 1923.

Crowley, Francis Keble. *A New History of Australia*. Australia: Heinemann, 1974.

Crowther, Sir William. 'Biographical Notes for the Frederick Smithies Exhibition'. Tasmania: State Library of Tasmania, 1977.

Devlin-Glass, Frances and Comte, Annette. *Flying 'In Between': Literature and Feminist Theory Since 'Frankenstein'*. Geelong: Deakin University, 1997.

De Vries, Susanna. 'Ethel Florence Lindesay (Henry Handel) Richardson', *Great Australian Women From Federation to Freedom*. Australia: Harper Collins, 2001, pp. 215–248.

Discover Mornington Peninsula. 'Fascinating Historic Facts: Mornington Peninsula Paddle Steamers of Port Philip Bay'. www.discovermorningtonpeninsula.com.au/fascinatingfacts/paddle-steamers.php.

Dropulich, Silvia. 'Silencing Women'. *Voice, The Age*, July 2010.

Durham, Carolyn A. *The Contexture of Feminism, Marie Cardinal and Multicultural Literacy*. USA: University of Illinois Press, 1992.

'Elegance in Wood', Queenscliff Diary. Victoria: Ministry of Planning and Environment, 1988.

Ewart, Rhonda and Brennan, Janette. 'Golden girls. A celebration of our centenarian alumni'. *Alumni News*. Australia: UTAS. December 2010, pp. 4–5.

Fitch, Joanna. *Beyond the Garden Gate: Local insight into the Victorian female suffrage movement*. Australia: Victorian Women's Trust, 2009.

Fitzpatrick, Theodora. *Some Reflections*. Tasmania: The Examiner Press, 1947.

Flint, Kate. 'Introduction' and 'Notes' in *The Waves*, by Virginia Woolf, 1932. England: Penguin Books, 1992.

Goldstein, Vida. *Women's Suffrage in Australia*. Australia: Victorian Women's Trust, 2008.

Greer, Germaine. 'Change is a feminist issue'. *The Age*. Comments and Debate. 8 March 2010, p. 11.

Grinter, Patrick. *I Build Boats*. Queensland: Zipprint, 2005.

Hadary, Sharon and Henderson, Laura. *How Women Lead: The 8 Essential Strategies Successful Women Know*. New York: McGraw Hill, 2013.

Hawley, Janet. *Artists in Conversation*. Richmond, Victoria: The Slattery Media Group Pty. Ltd., 2012.

Hawthorn, Jeremy. *A Concise Glossary of Contemporary Literary Theory: Second Edition*. London: Arnold, 1994.

Hill, Barry. *The Enduring Rip: A History of Queenscliffe*. Melbourne: Melbourne University Press, 2004.

Holmes, Diana and Tarr, Carrie. *A 'Belle Epoque'? Women in French Society and Culture 1890–1914*. New York: Berghahn Books, 2006.

Knightley, Phillip. *Australia*. London: Jonathan Cape, 2000.

Lake, Marilyn. *Getting Equal: The History of Australian Feminism*. Australia: Allen & Unwin, 1999.

Loney, Jack. *Wrecks Along the Great Ocean Road*. Australia: Marine History Publications, 1967.

Longmire, Anne. *The Catalysts: Change and Continuity 1910–2010*. Australia: Anne Longmire and The Catalysts, 2011.

Moi, Toril. *Sexual Textual Politics*. London: Routledge, 1985.

Queenscliffe Urban Conservation Study. The Ministry for Planning Victoria. Geelong Regional Commission. Allom, Lovell & Associates Pty. Ltd. Architects. Reference No. 98, 1982, p. 179.

Ramazani, Jahan. *Poetry of Mourning: The Elegy from Hardy to Heaney*. Chicago: University of Chicago Press, 1994.

Richardson, Henry Handel. *Ultima Thule*. Australia: Penguin Books, 1971.

Richardson, Henry Handel. *Myself When Young*. Great Britain: William Heinemann, 1948.

Richardson, Walter and Mary. *The Letters of Walter and Mary Richardson*. Elizabeth Webby and Gillian Sykes (ed.), Australia: The Miegunyah Press, 2000.

Sentinel Advertisers 1882–1919. Queenscliff. p. 177.

Schnackenberg, Sally. *Kate Weindorfer: The Woman Behind the Man on the Mountain*. Tasmania: Regal Publications, 1995.

Smithies, Frederick. 'Rugged Crags, Nature's Challenge to the Mountaineer'. *The Examiner Annual*. Launceston, Tasmania, 1935.

Smithies, Frederick, 'Skyline Climb on Cradle Mountain,' Tasmania, 1937.

'The History of the Ozone Hotel Queenscliff'. *Queenscliffe Historical Museum Book Series*. vol. 2, Queenscliffe Historical Museum Inc., 2003.

Victorian Heritage Database. www.vhd.heritage.vic.gov.au/places/heritage/4826.

Waight, Sarah. 'Women's bushwalking and outdoor activities'. Rosaline Stephensen interview. National Museum of Australia, 28 January 1993.

Wolf, Naomi. *Fire With Fire: The New Female Power And How It Will Change the 21st Century*. London: Chatto & Windus, 1993.

Woods, Carole. 'Fellows, Thomas Howard (1822–1878)', *Australian Dictionary of Biography*, vol. 4. Australia: Melbourne University Press, 1972.

Wynd, Ian. 'Mannerim', *Balla-wein: A History of the Shire of Bellarine*. Victoria: The Council of the Shire of Bellarine, 1988.

The Authors

Helen Downey

The career of non-fiction author Helen Downey mirrors the familiar pattern of work for many women. Helen's promising start, with four books in her *History on Stage* series, published in quick succession, was put on hold after the arrival of three children.

Helen holds a Bachelor of Education and TSTC at Melbourne State College, with a major in Asian Fine Arts and Sculpture, and a Bachelor of Letters (Honours) at Deakin University, with a major in Myth and Ideology.

Helen has written feature stories for *The Age*, *Canberra Times*, *Sunday Herald* and *The Weekly Times*. Her *History on Stage* series includes the titles *Ancient America*; *Ancient River Civilizations, Suma and Egypt*; *Ancient Greece*; and *Ancient Rome*. She is the author of *Wide World of English* 2, and co-author of the Techne leaflet series for ACTA. She was an Editor and writer of 'Asthma Update' for the Asthma Foundations of Australia, and an Editor for the teachers' notes 'Challenge', 'Pursuit', 'Explore' and 'Comet'.

This former secondary art, media studies, history and English teacher was also a member of the Secondary Art and Craft Standing Committee, is an experienced Queenscliffe Information Centre Volunteer Heritage Guide, and recently returned from a year living in France

Her most current work, a biography of Theodora Fitzpatrick, grew into *Making Herstory*.

Lorraine Secen

Lorraine holds a Certificate of Business Studies (Law), a Diploma of Financial Planning, a Bachelor of Laws (Honours) and Specialist Accreditation 1998.

Growing up in the country fostered a love of nature and the outdoors. With forebears who engendered great pride in their Irish/English heritage going back to the 1850s in Australia, followed by marriage to a post-war Italian migrant, she maintains an ongoing interest in, and love of, people, their lives and their stories. Woven throughout life has been a great love of family, of photography, of nature, of music and of learning.